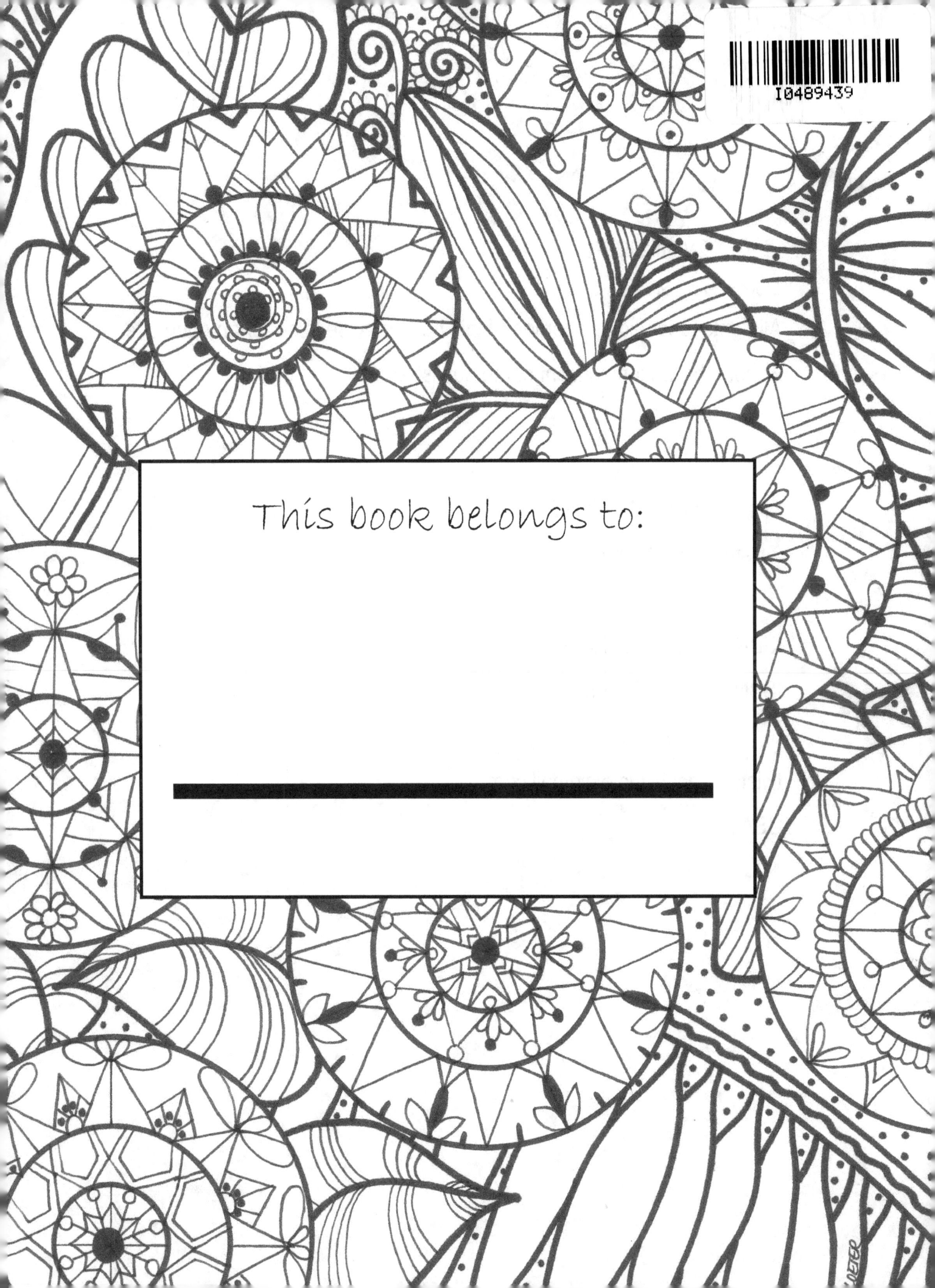

This book belongs to:

First Printing 2017, First Edition

Twisted Branch Studio

ISBN 13: 978-1548677909

ISBN 10-1548677906

twistedbranchstudio@gmail.com

USA

The proceeds from the sale of this book will go to support

Faith Children's Home

Santa Maria de Dota, San Jose, Costa Rica

https://www.faithministriescostarica.com/childrens-refuge

ONLINE DONATIONS

https://www.faithministriescostarica.com/donate

MAIL IN DONATIONS:

**Central Missionary Clearing House
P.O. Box 219228
Houston, TX 77218-9228**

Phone: (281) 599-7411

NOTE:

Please make checks payable to : **CMC**

Along with check please print and send in form for Church or Individual Donor found at this link:

https://www.faithministriescostarica.com/donate

Thank you and God bless!

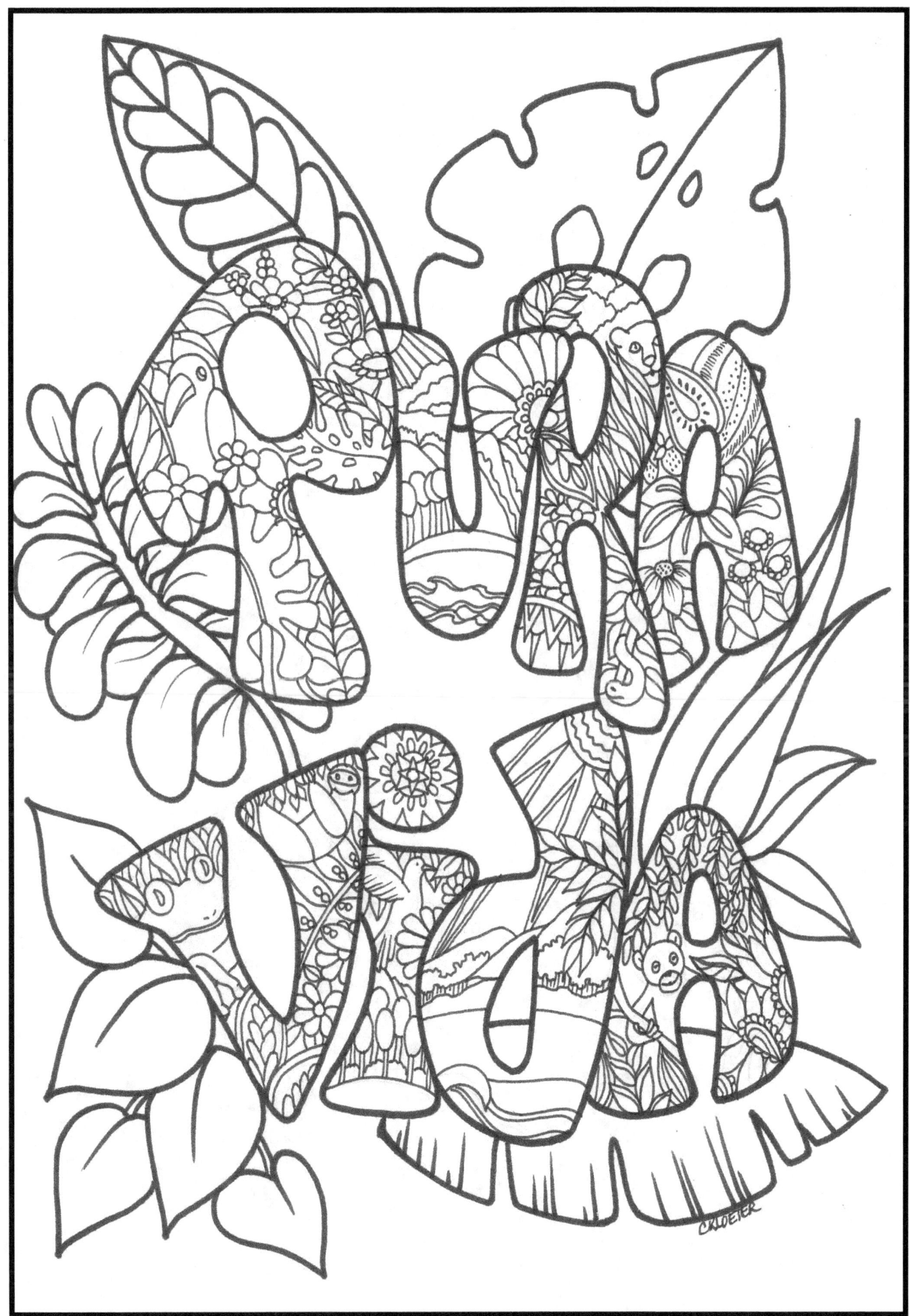

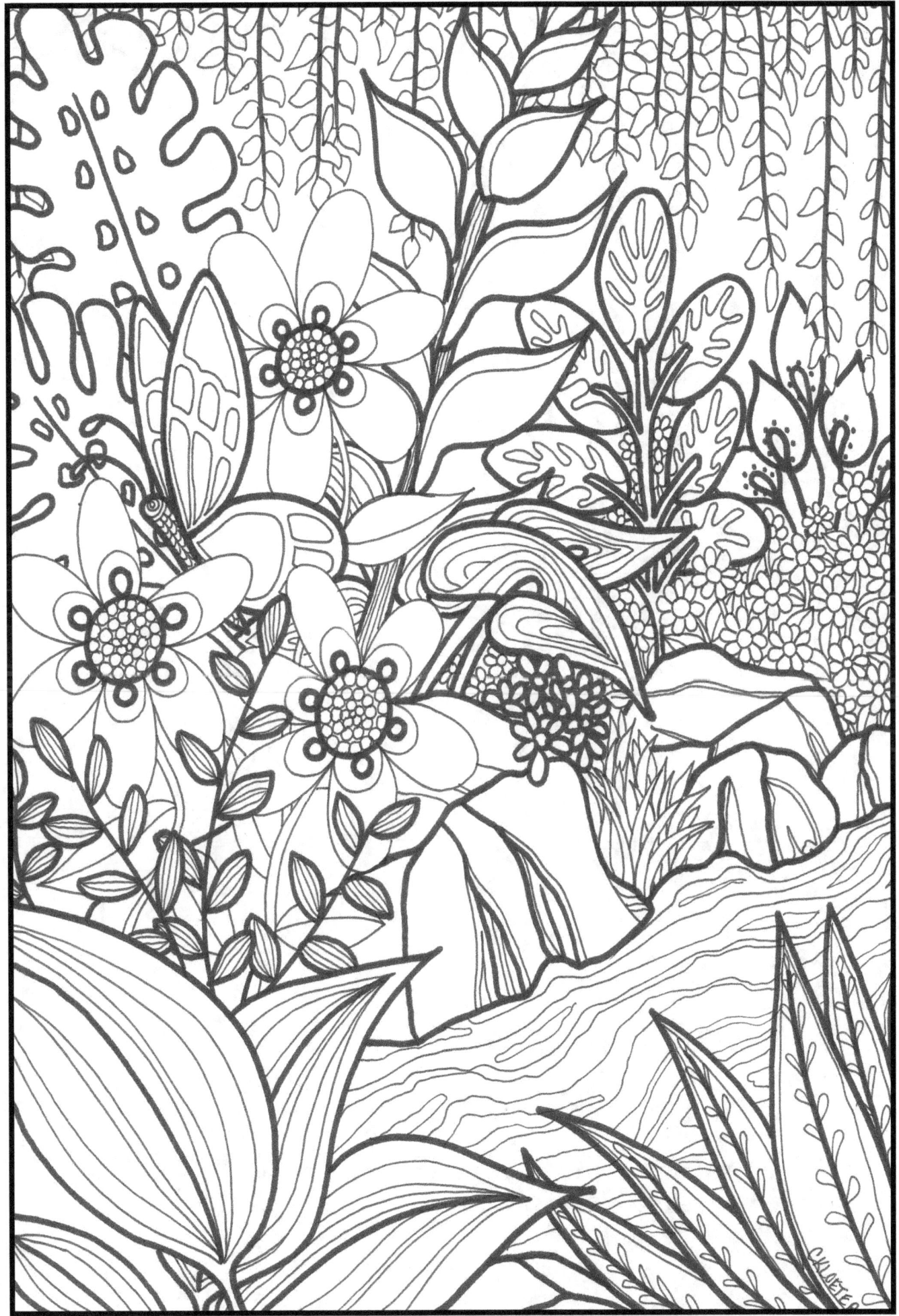

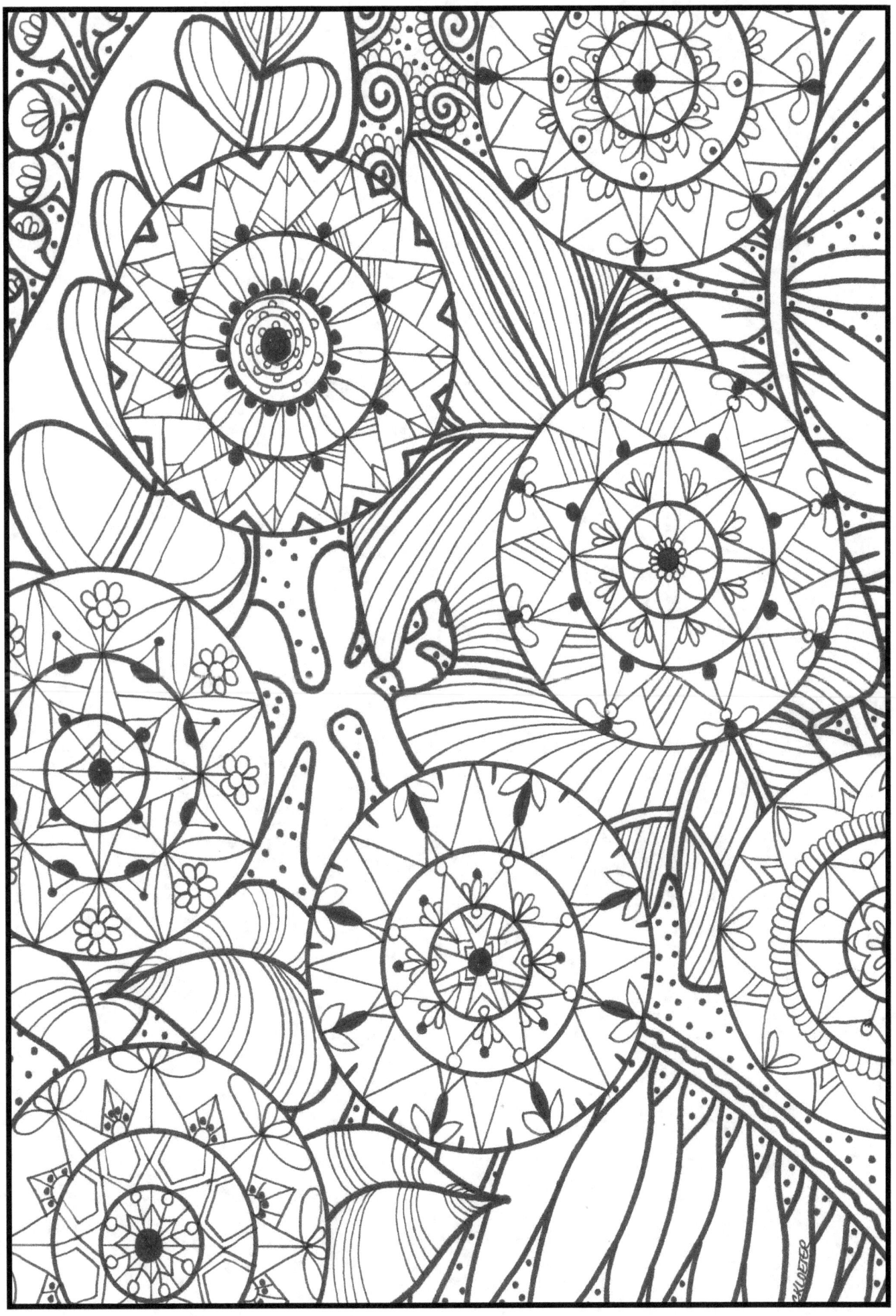

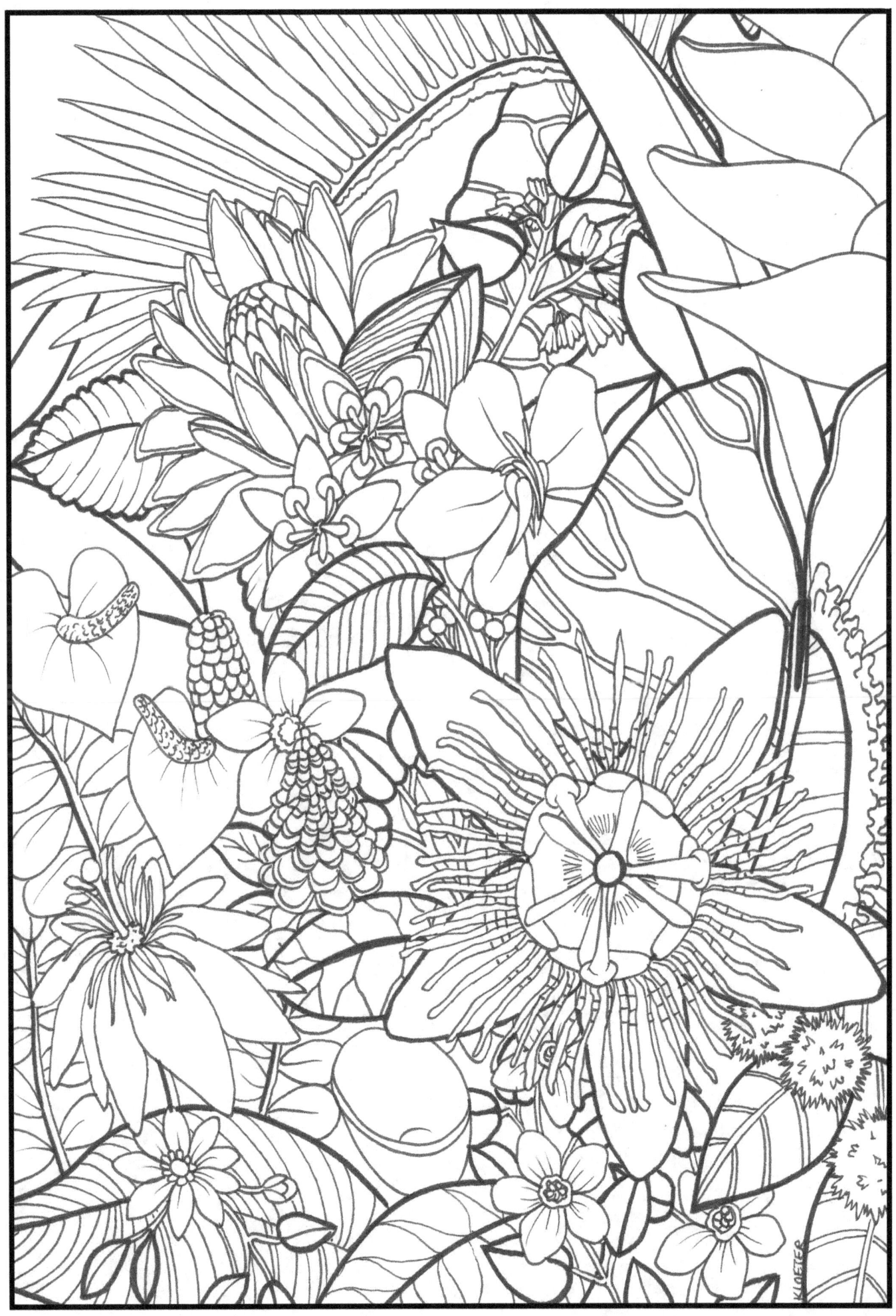

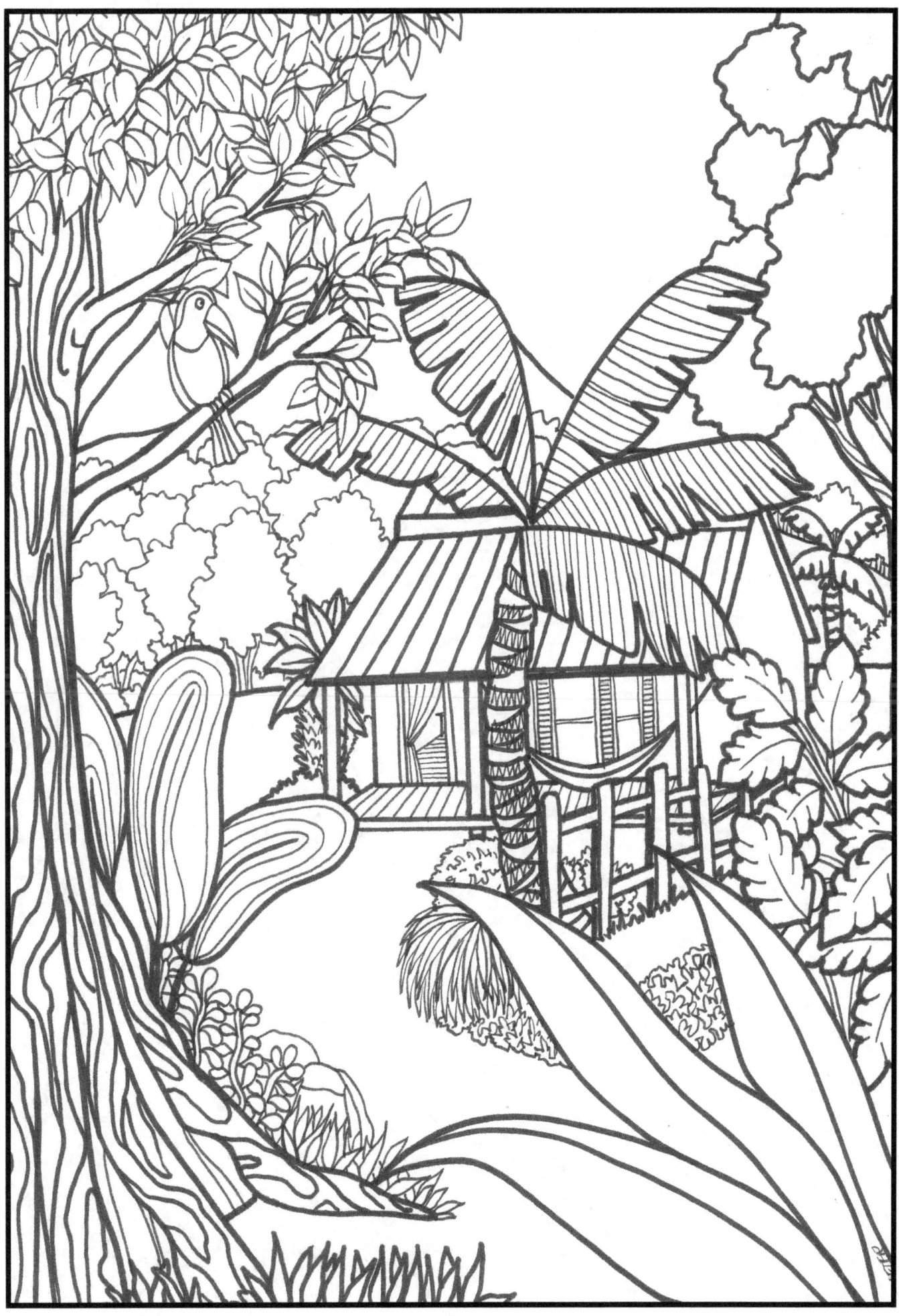

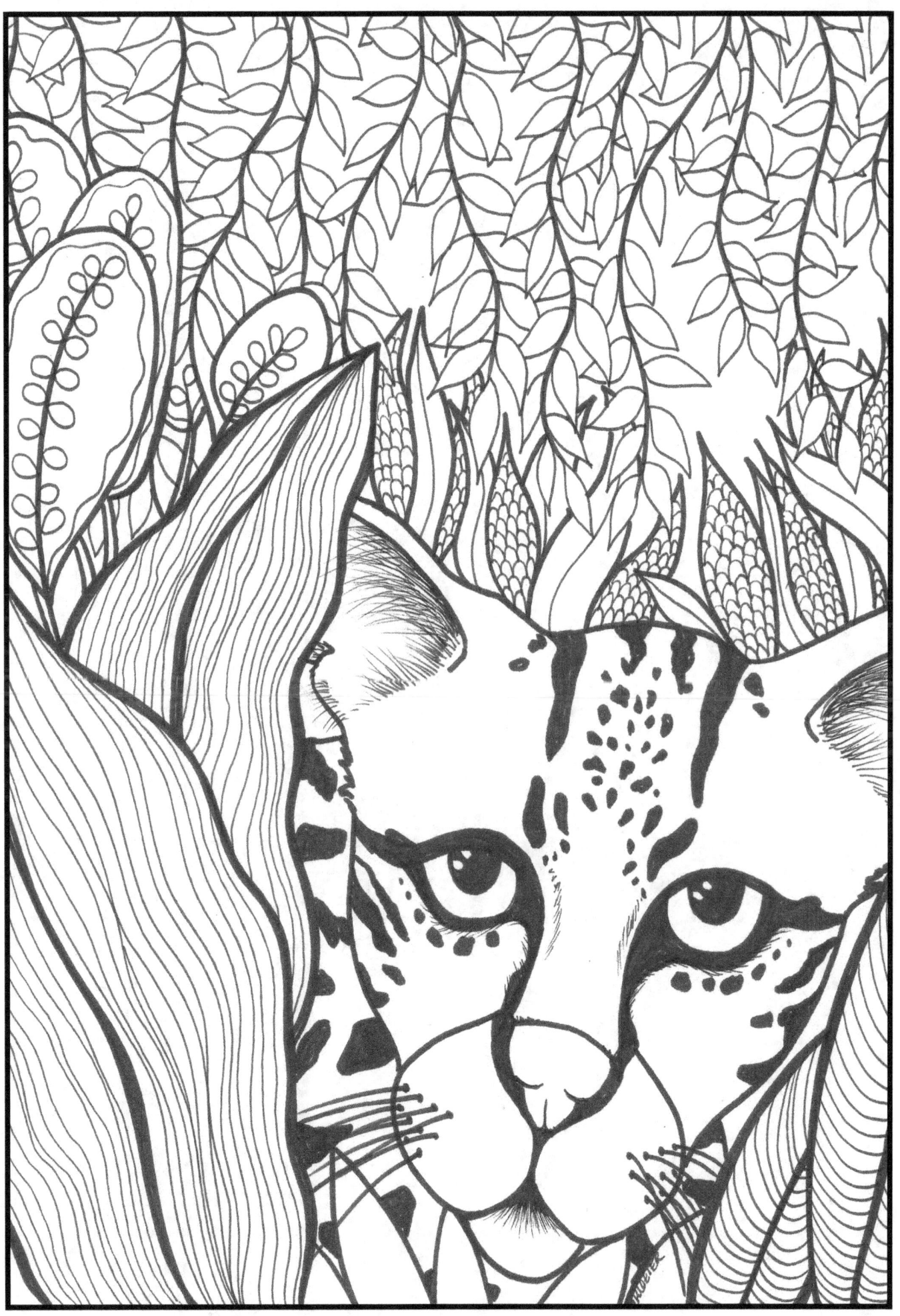

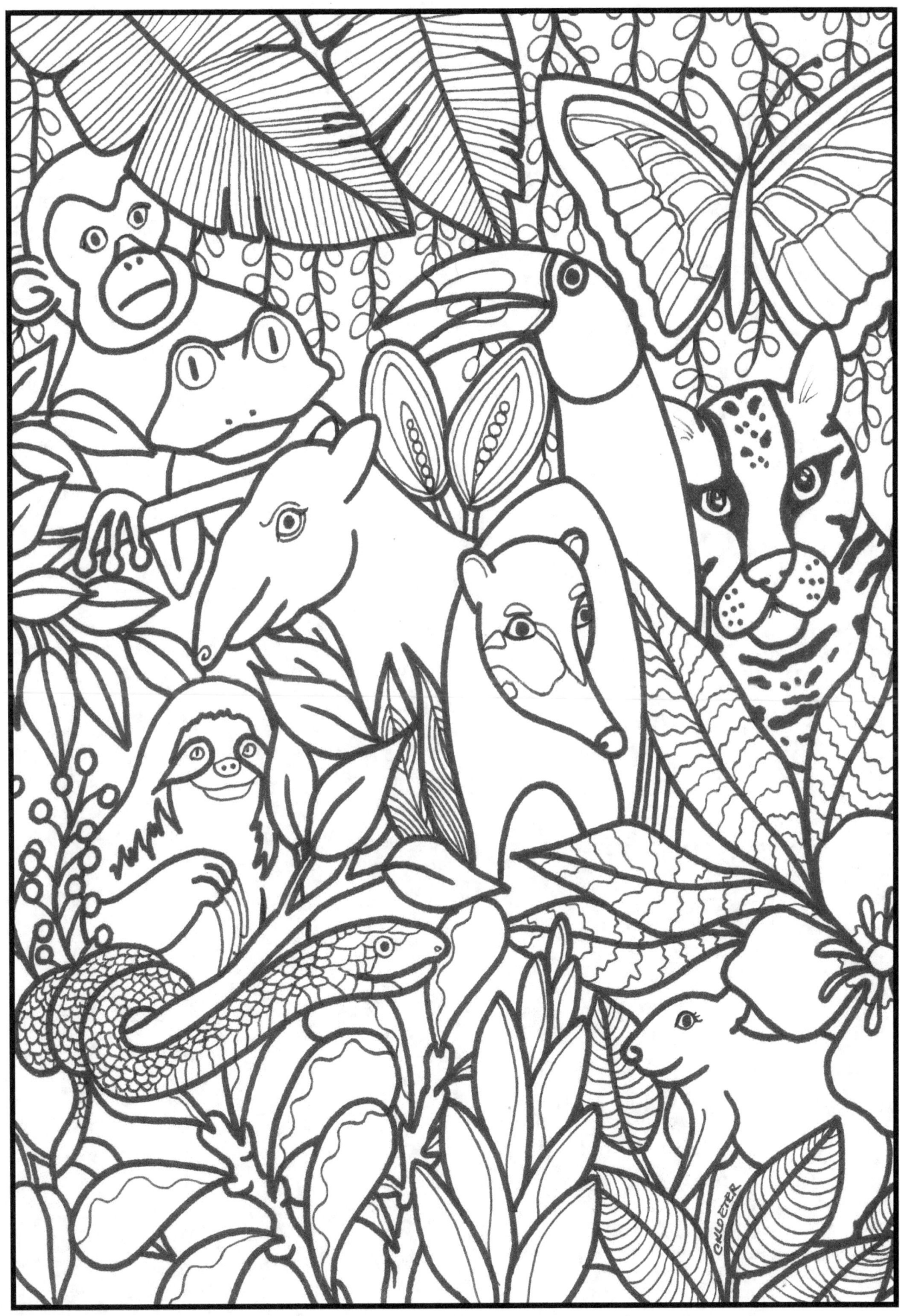

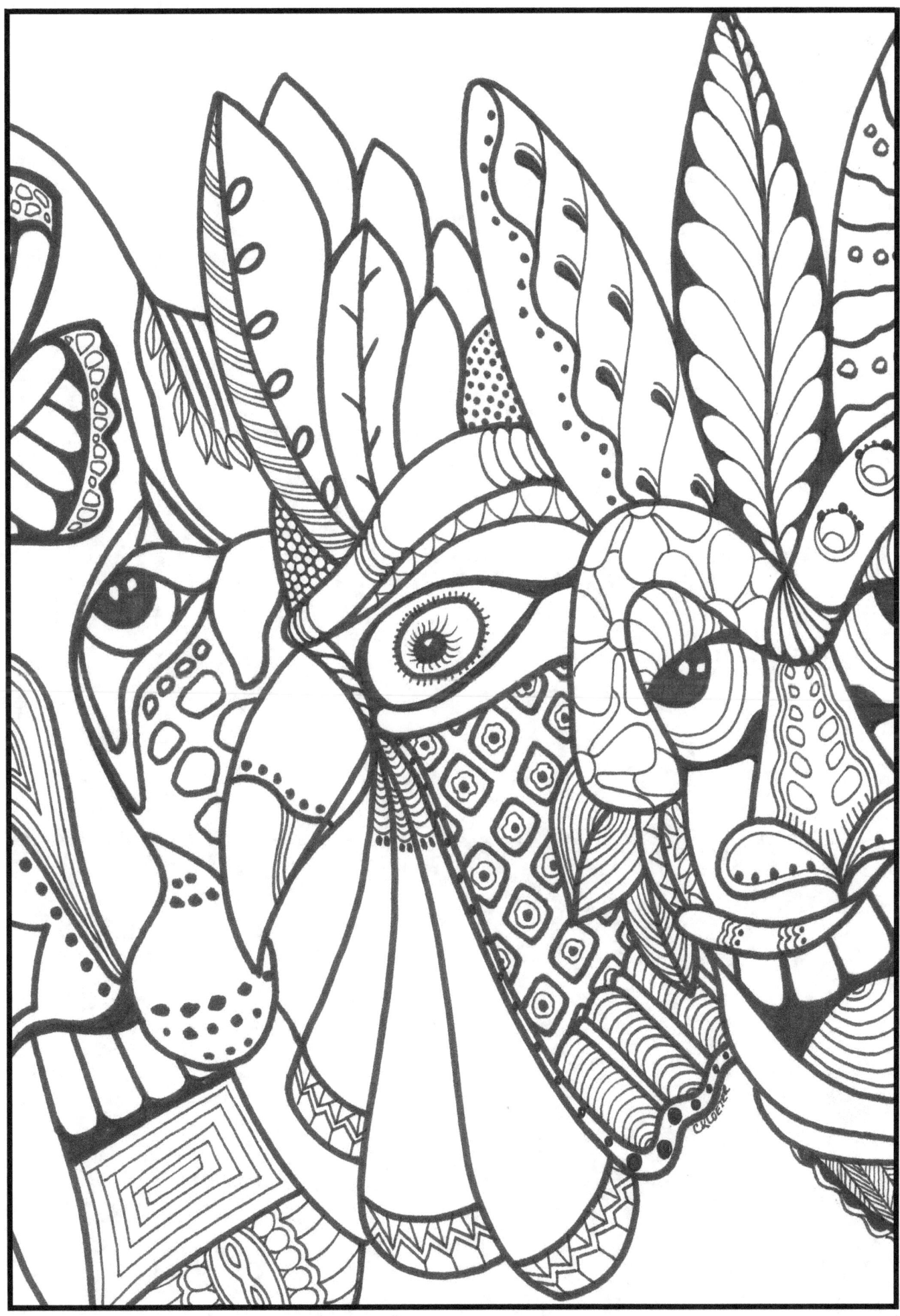

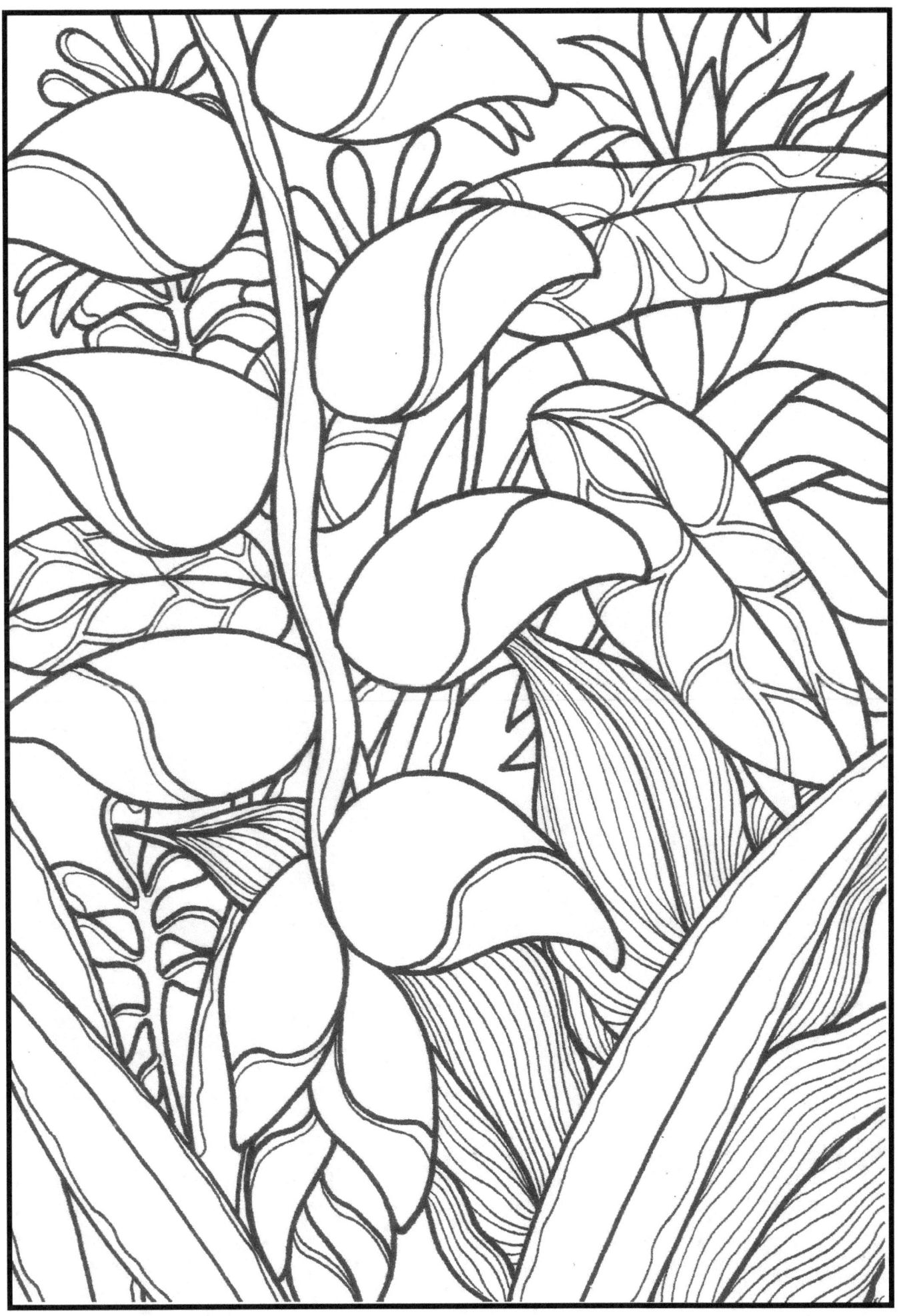

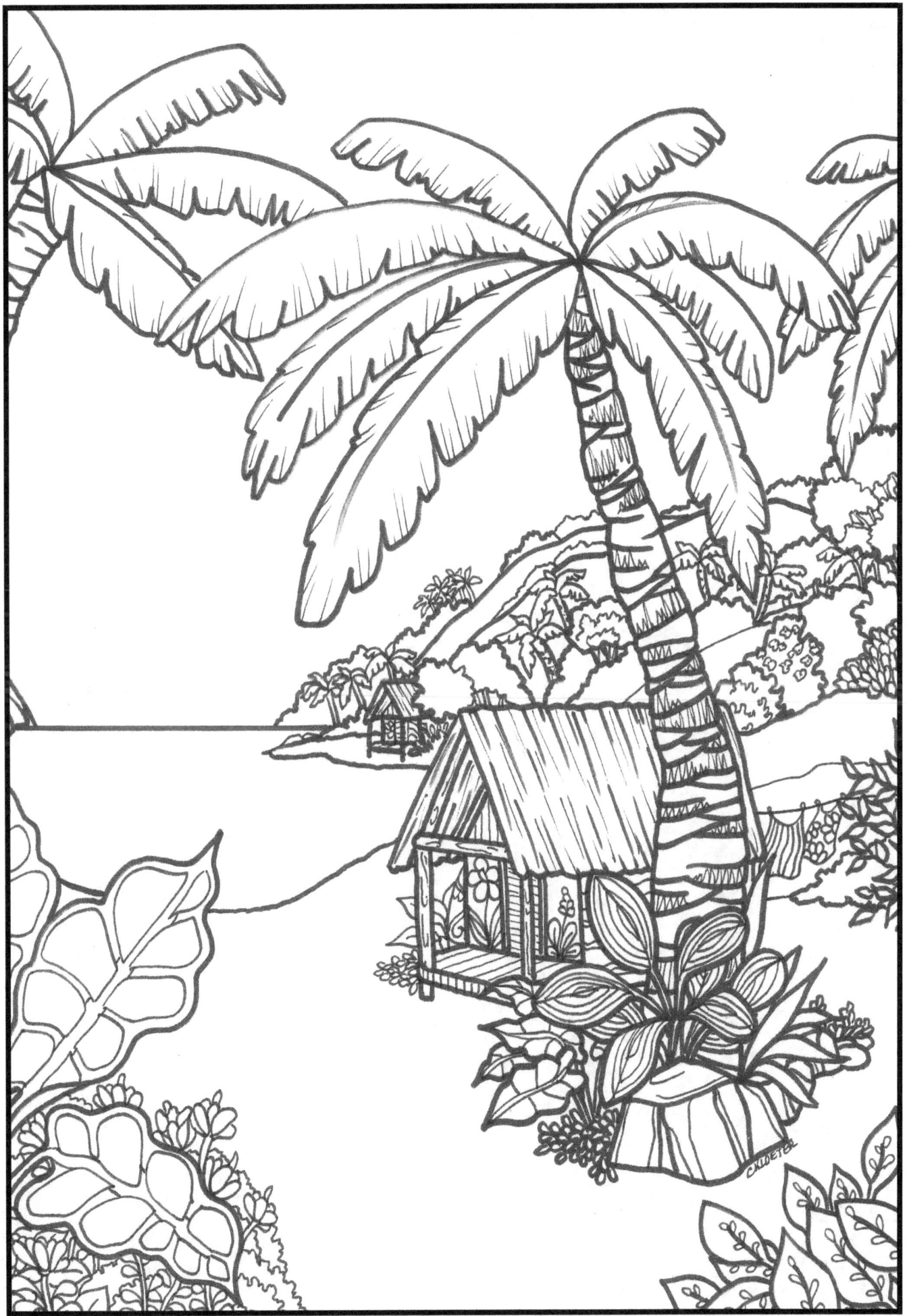

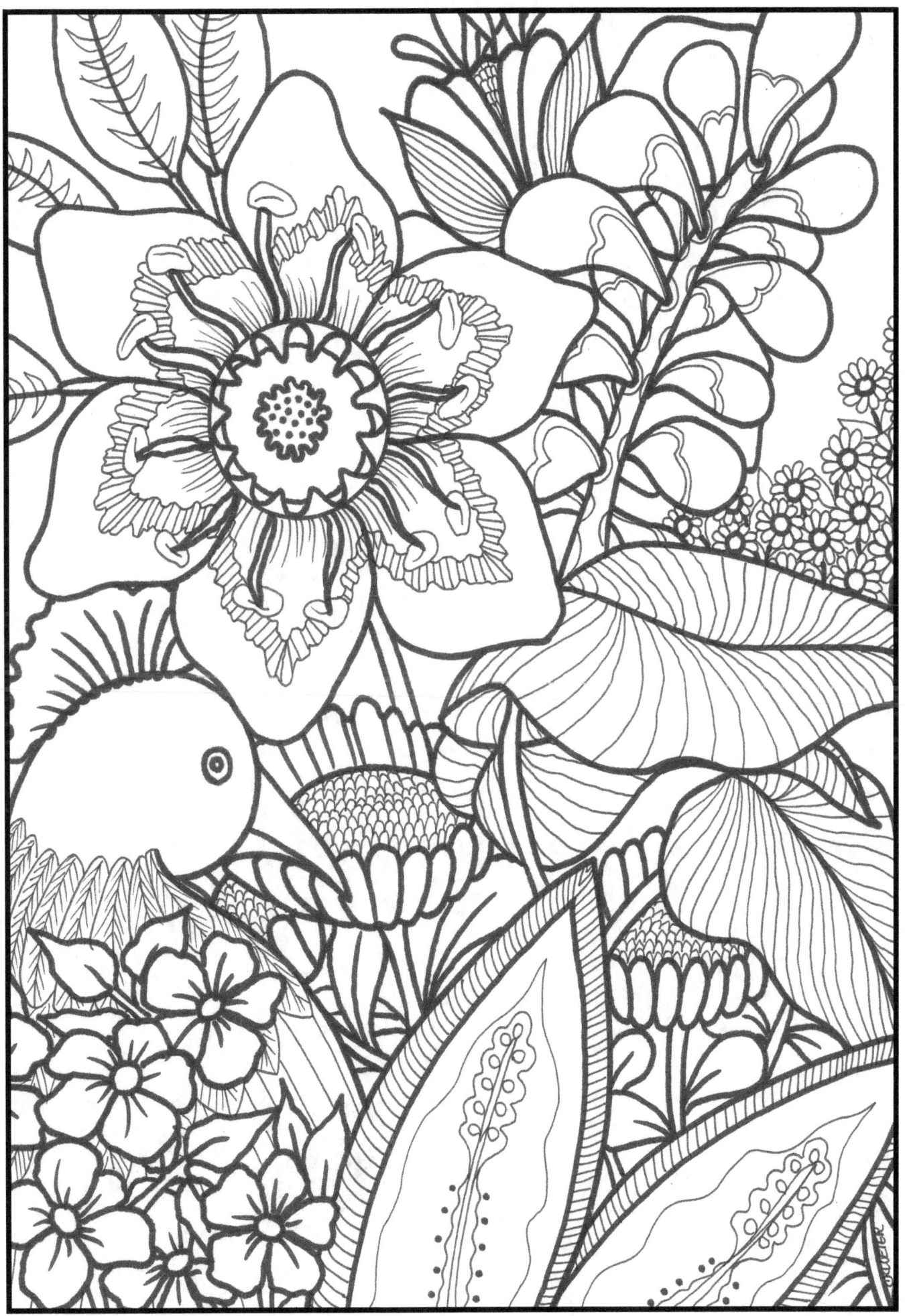

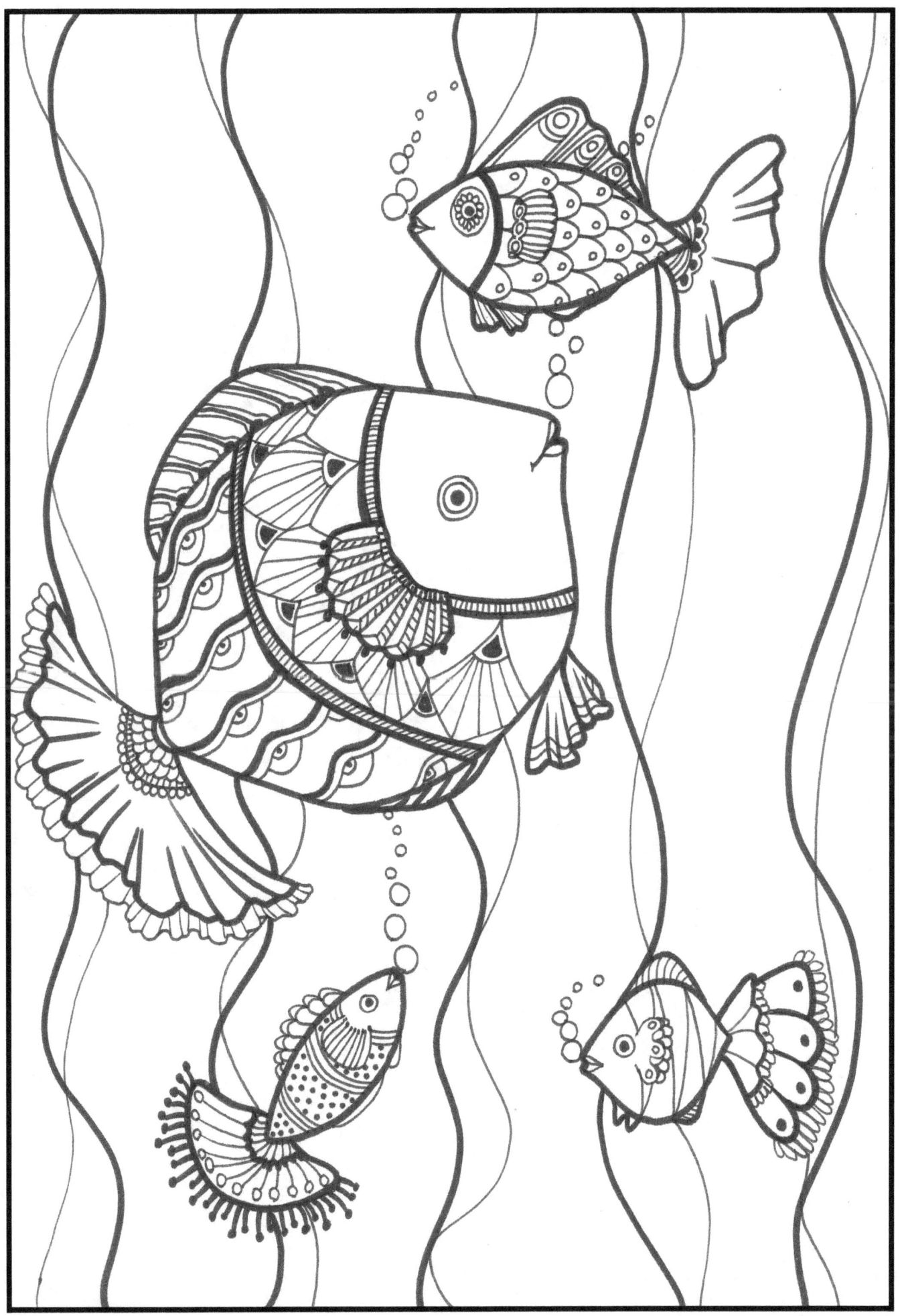

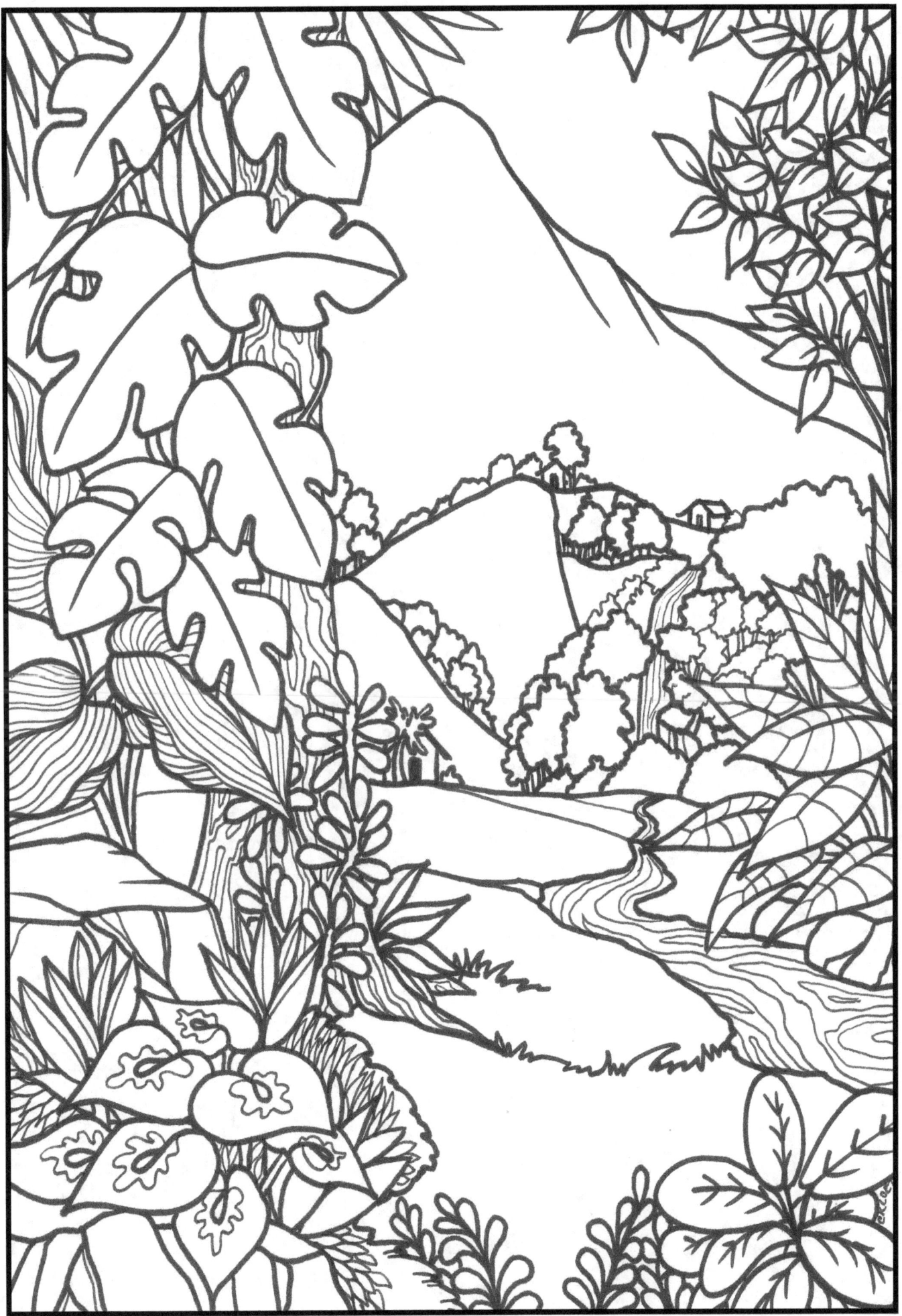

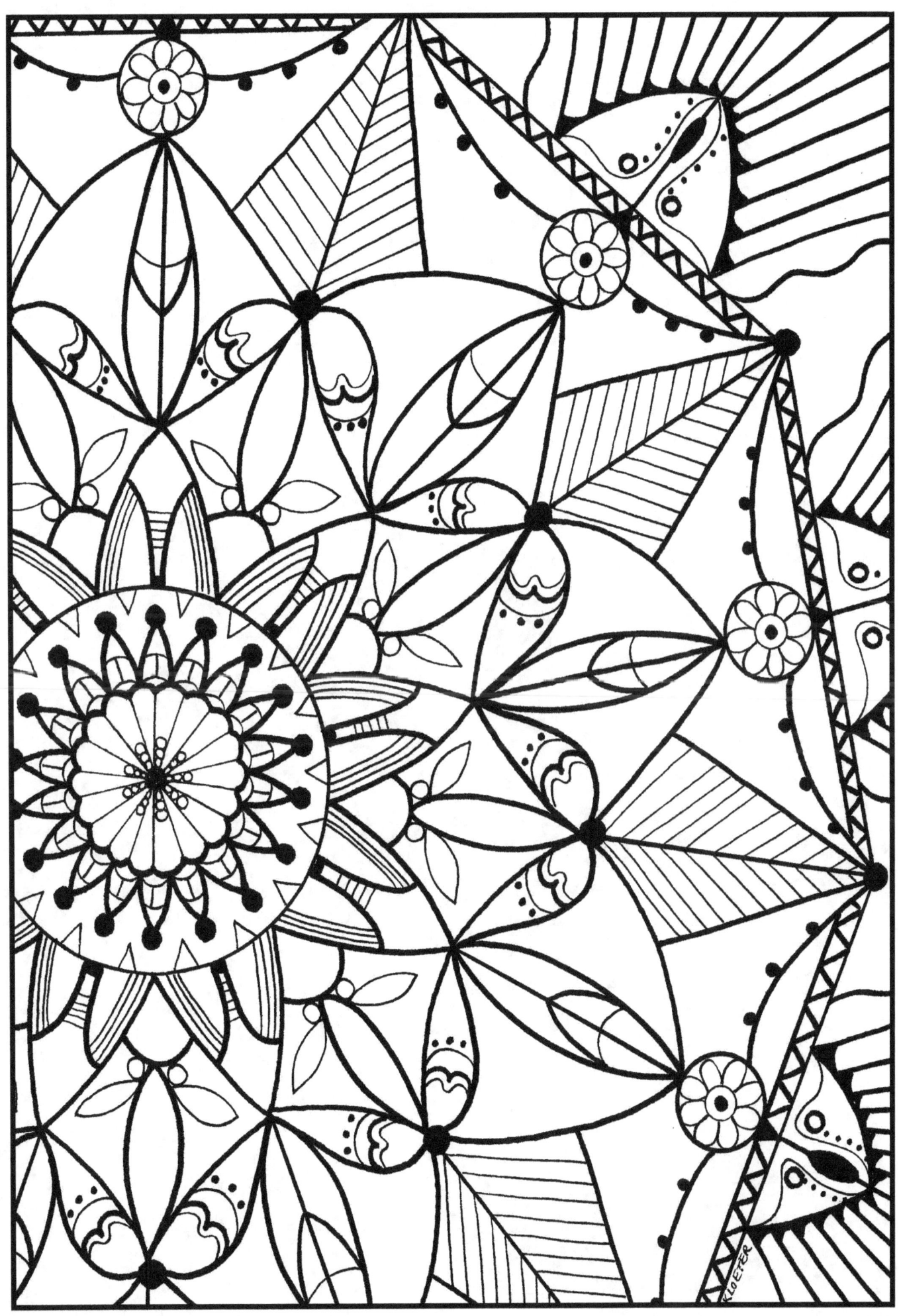

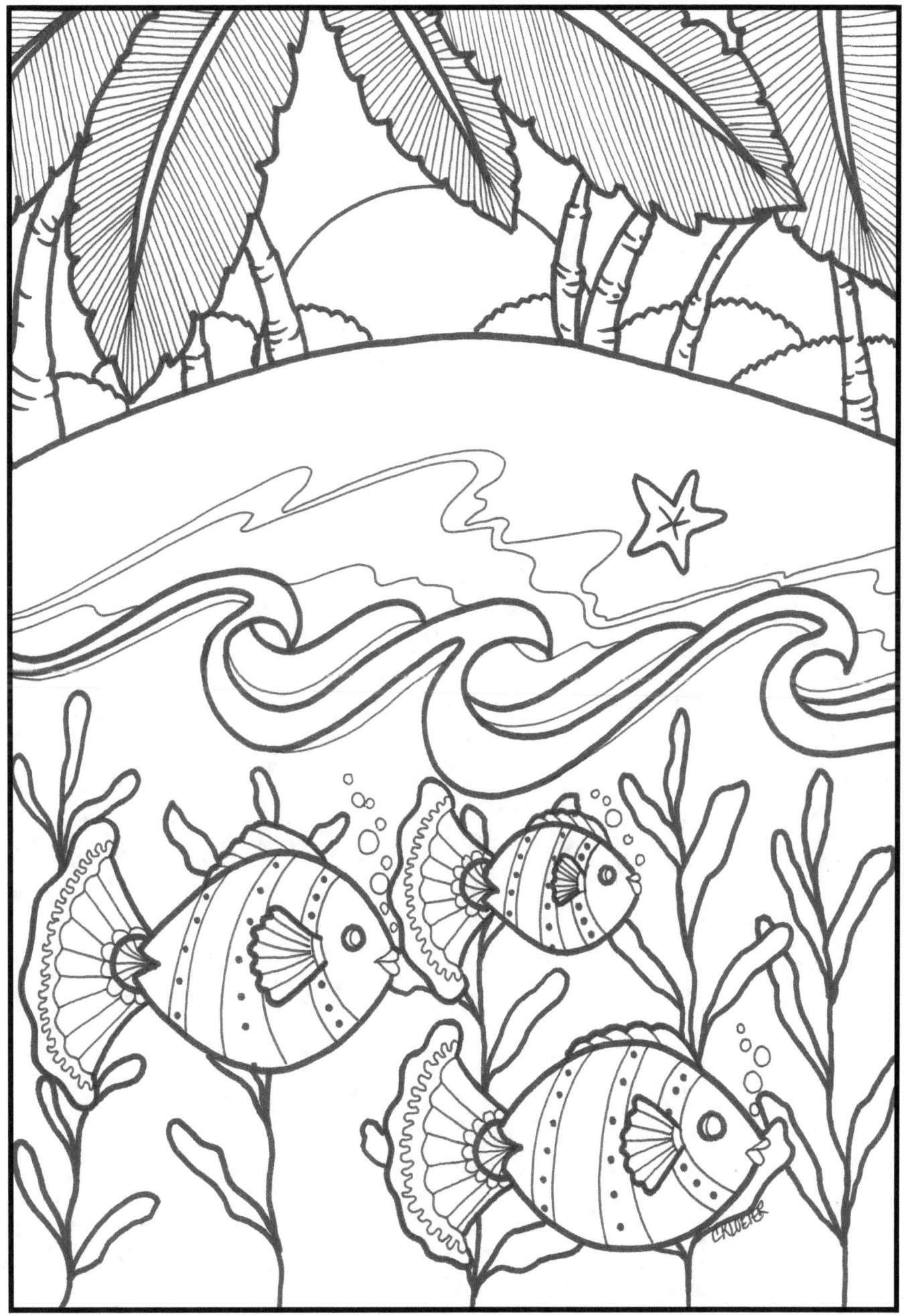

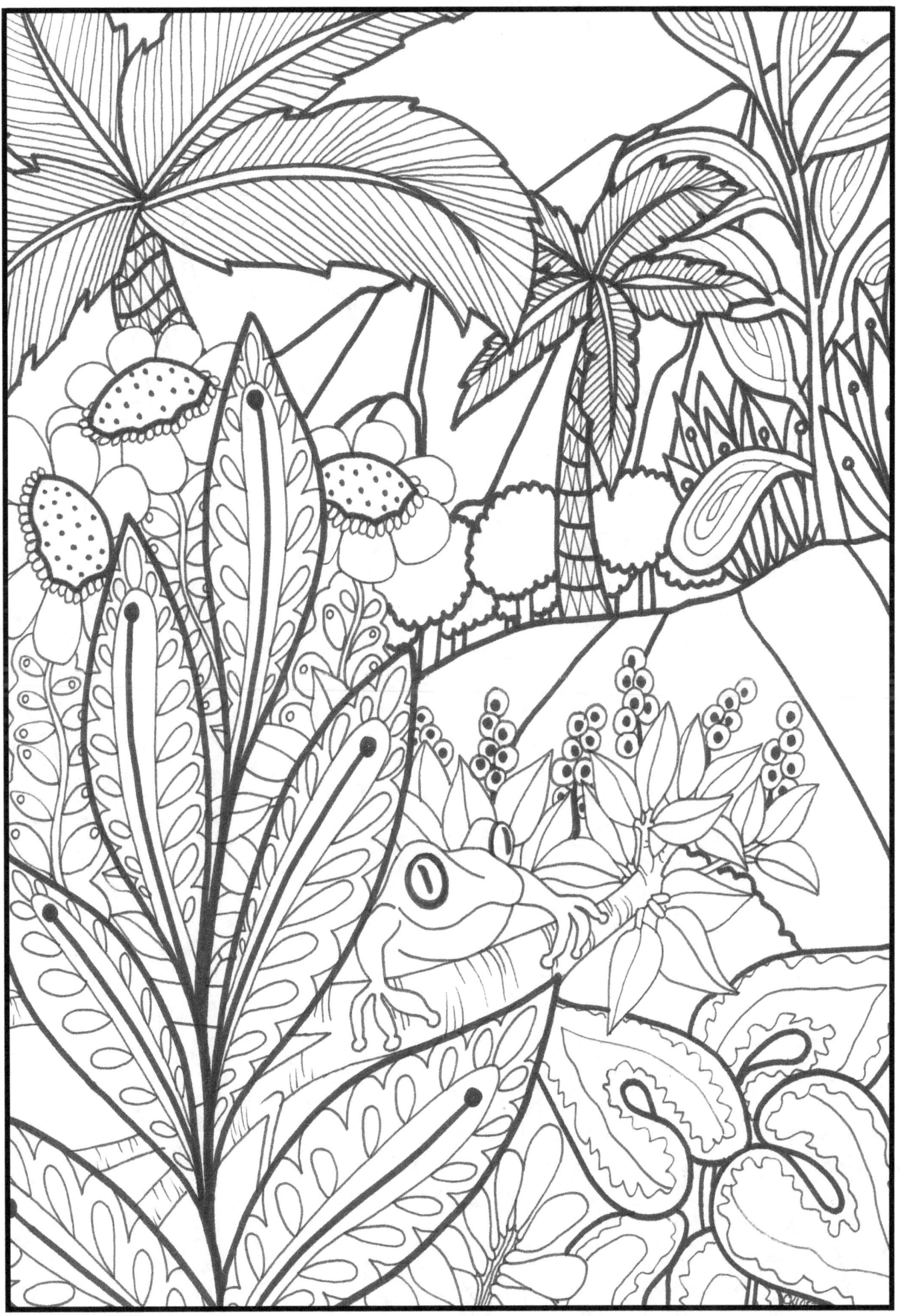

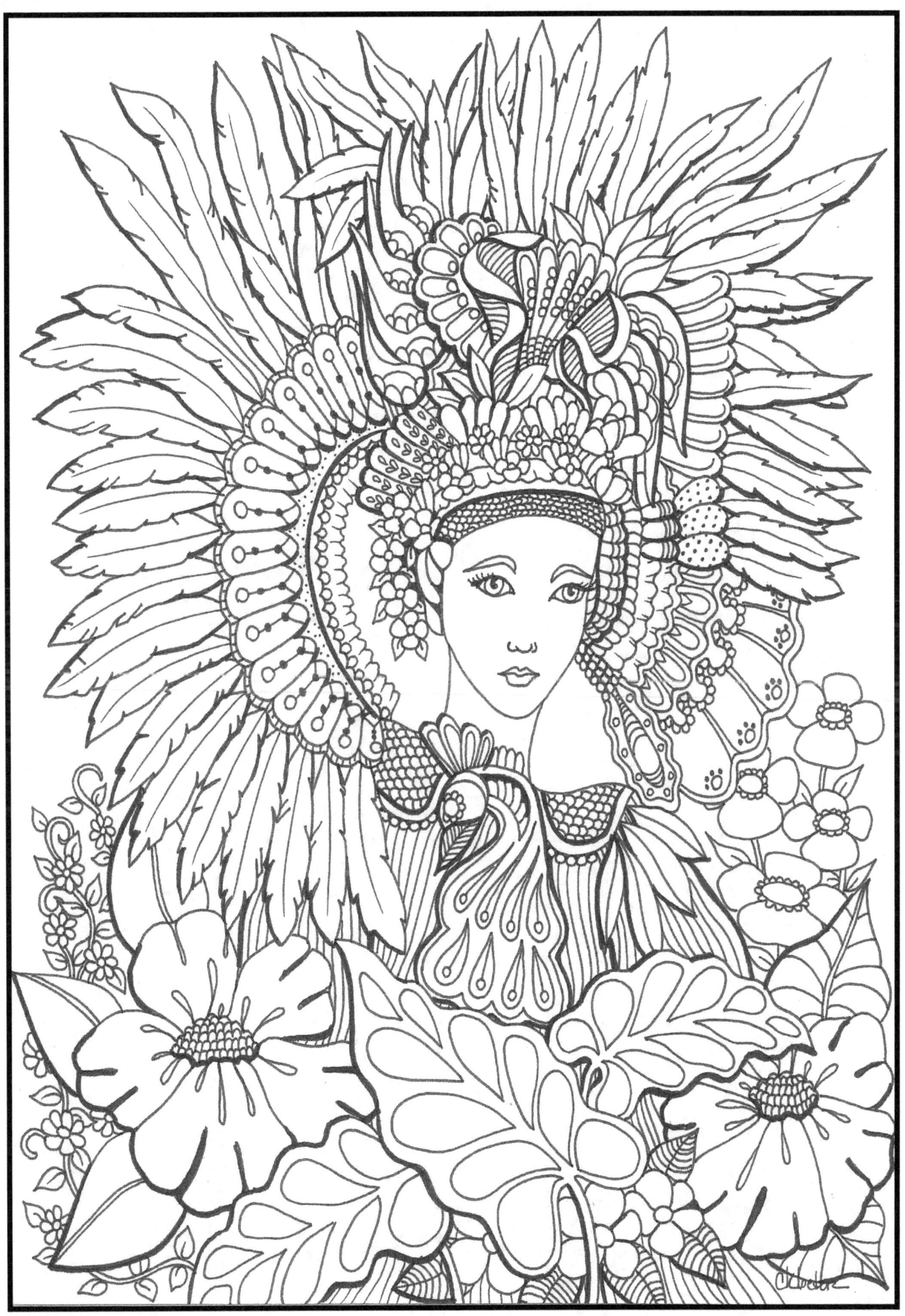

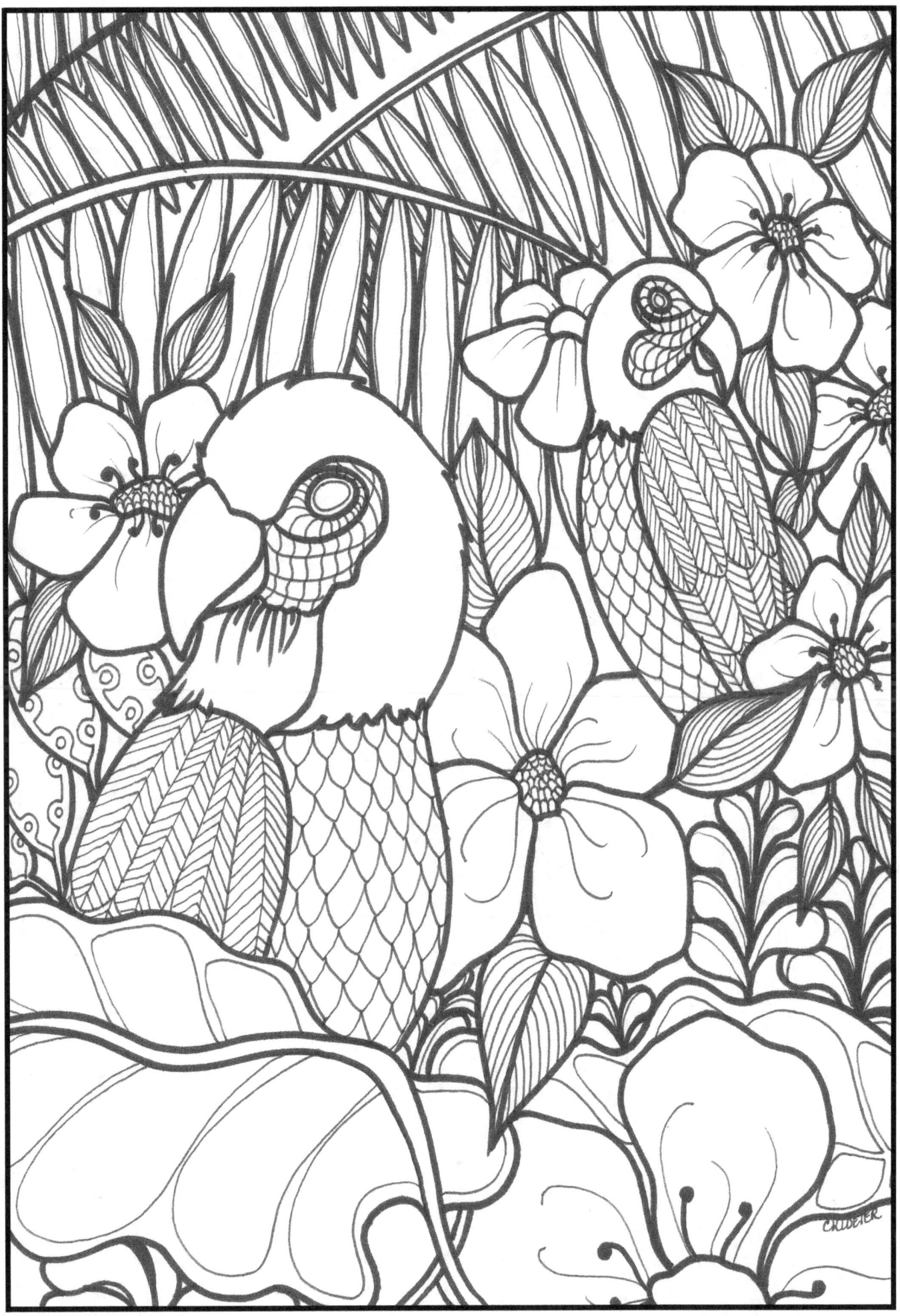

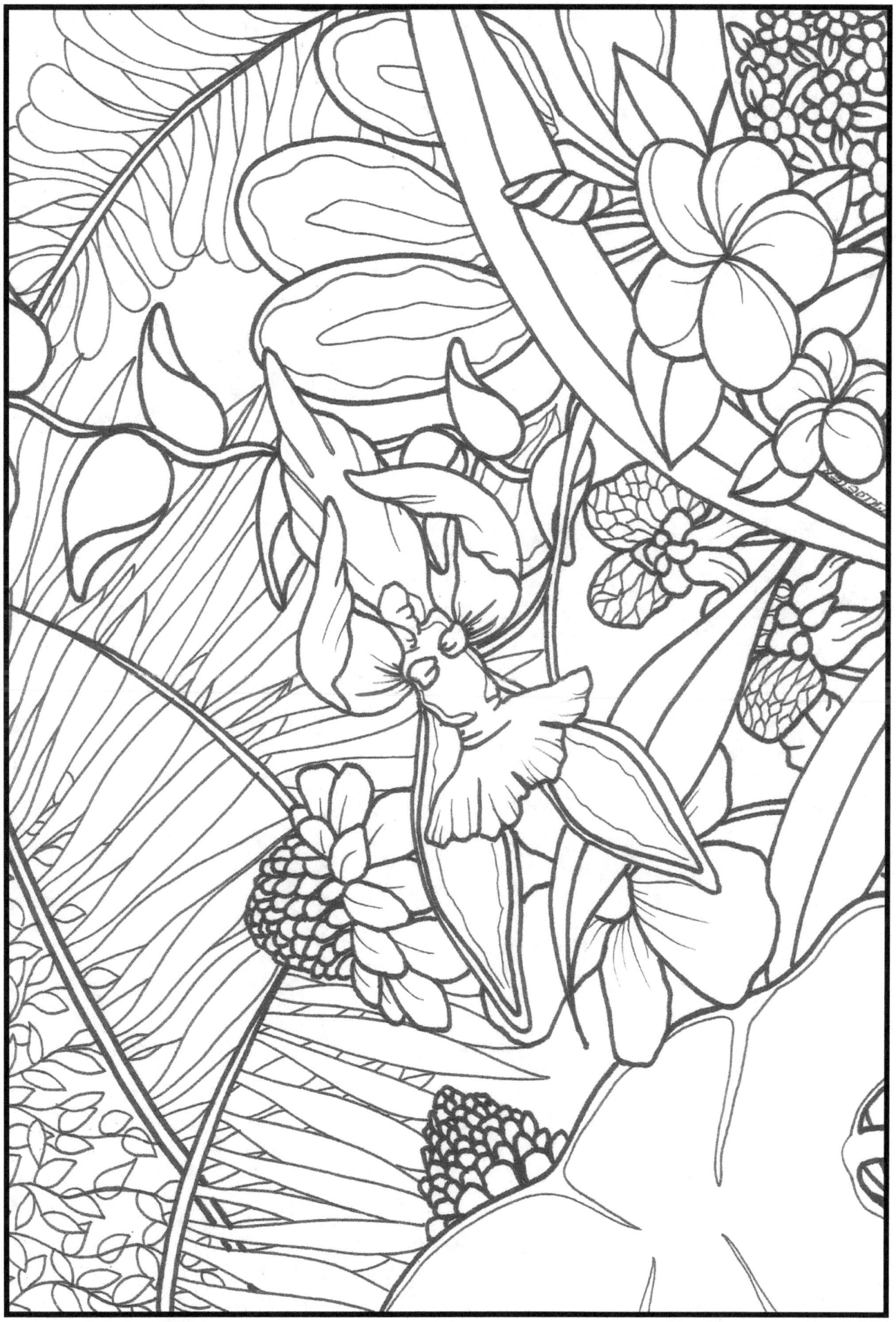

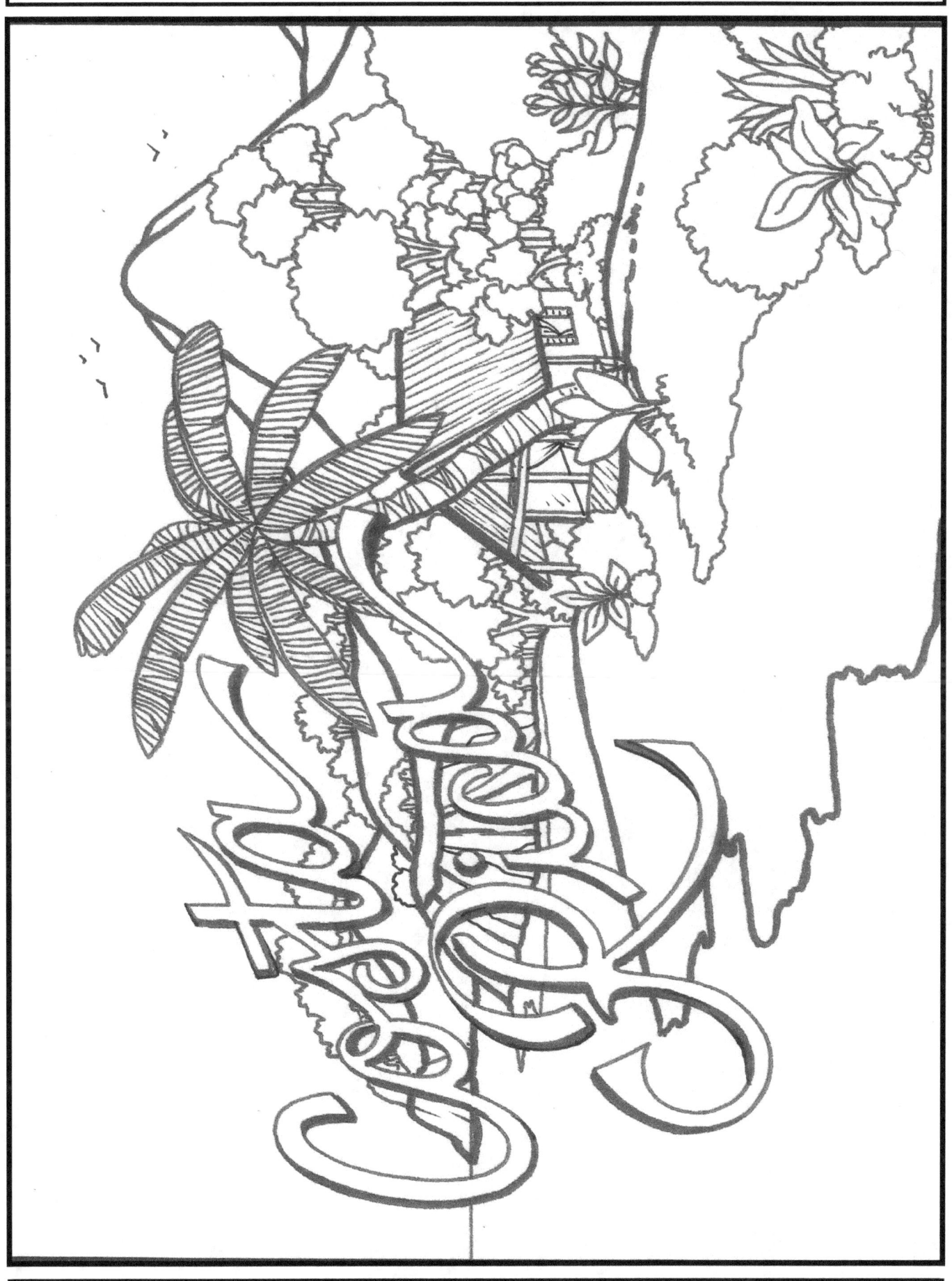

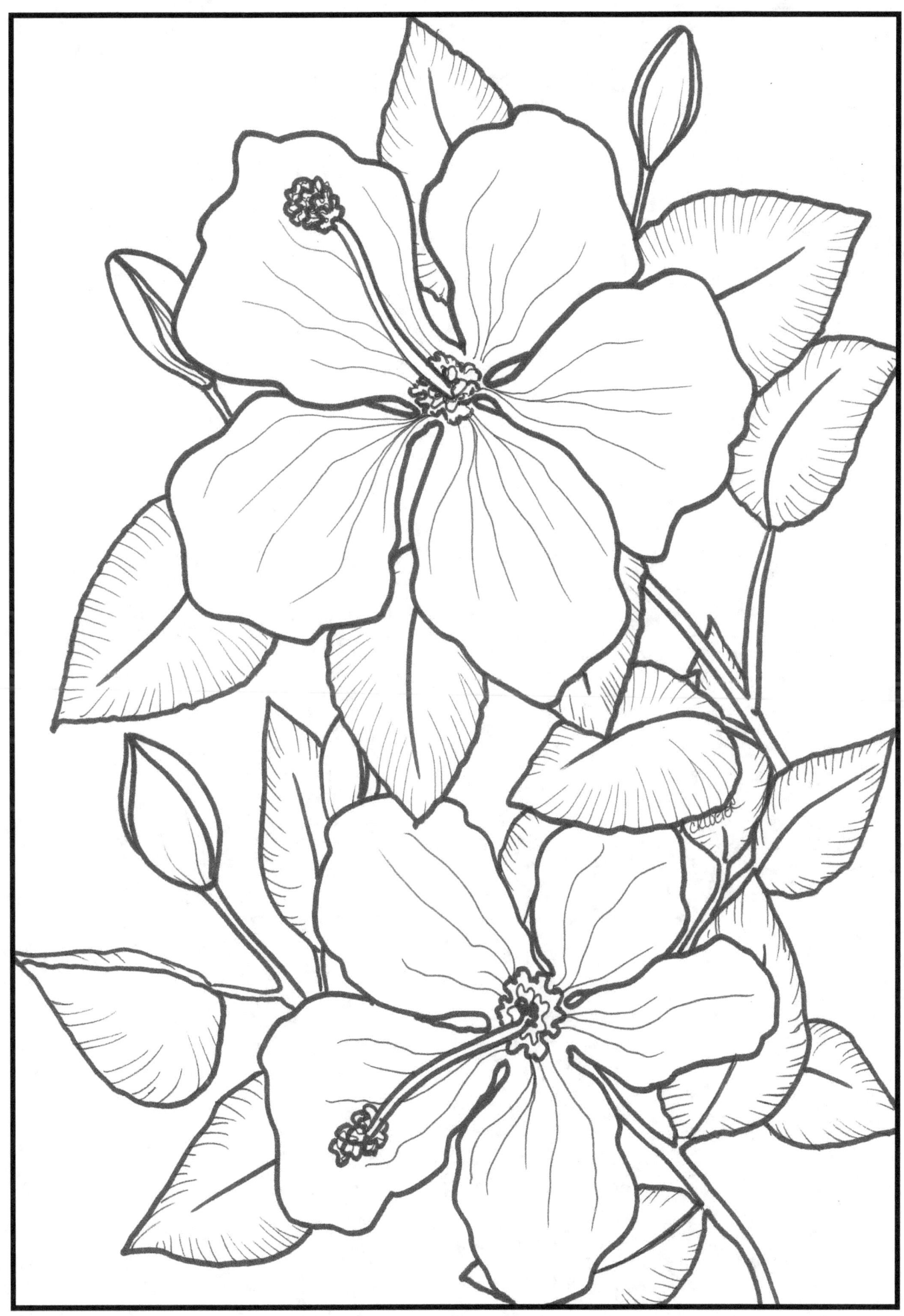

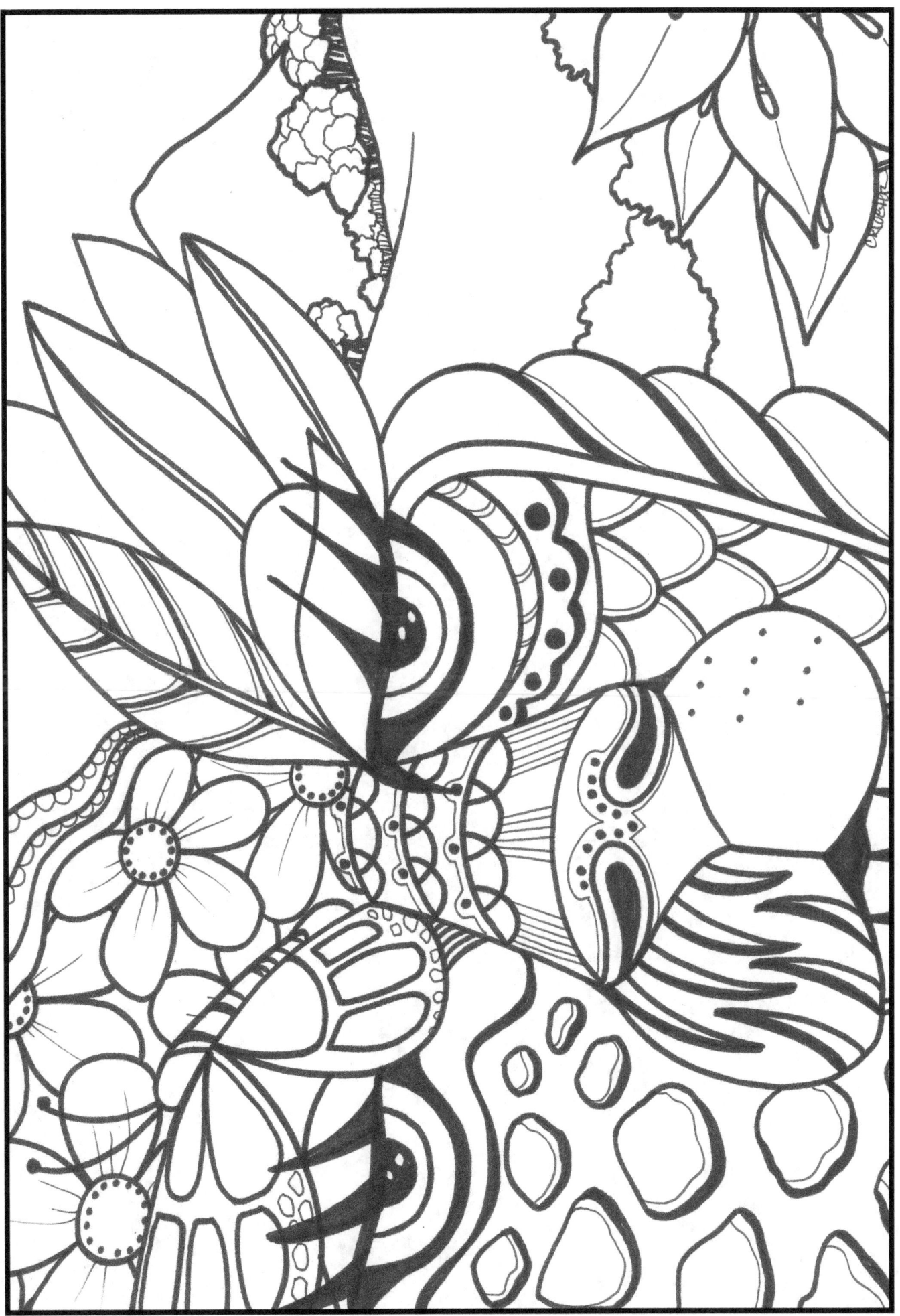

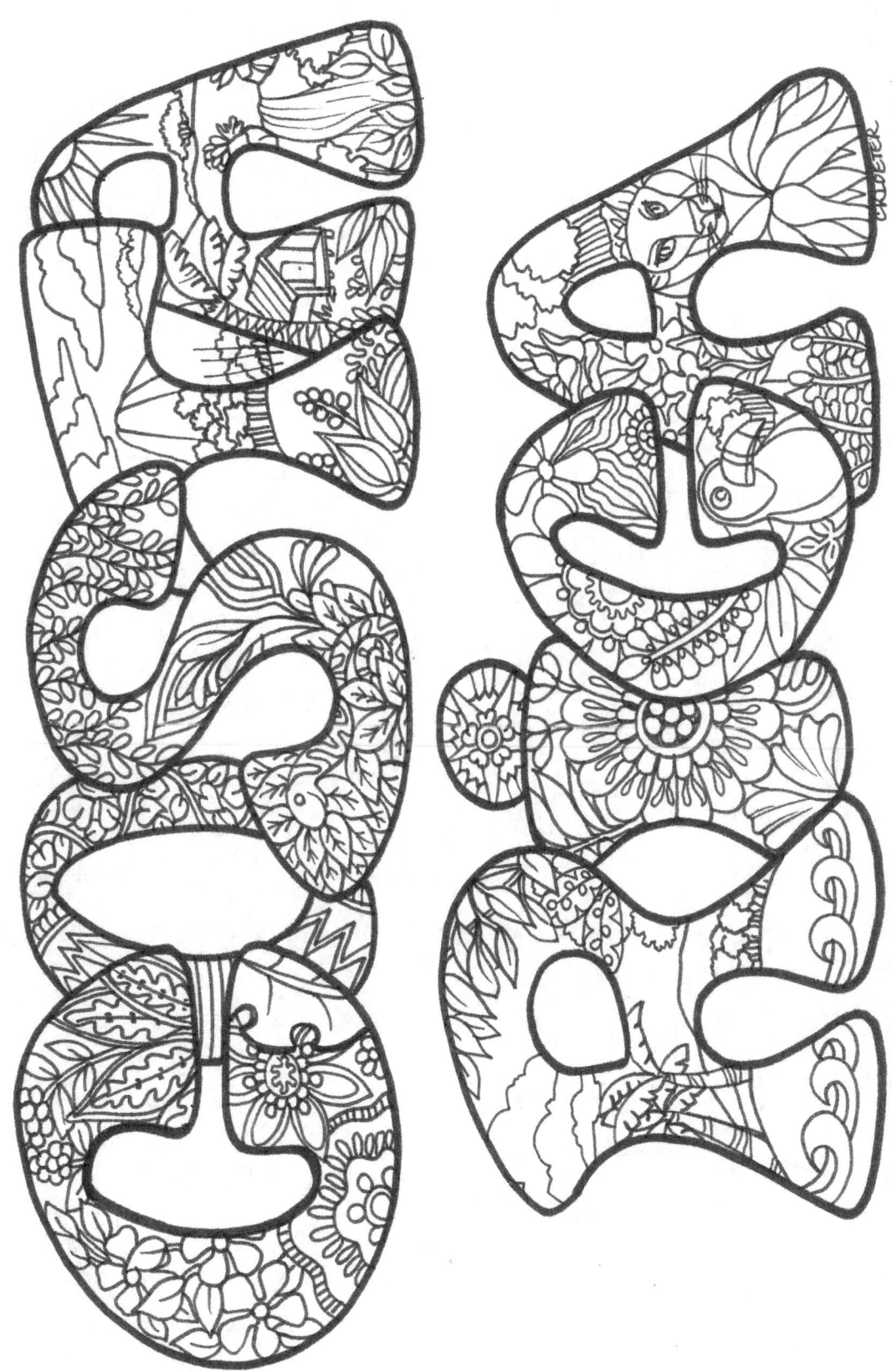

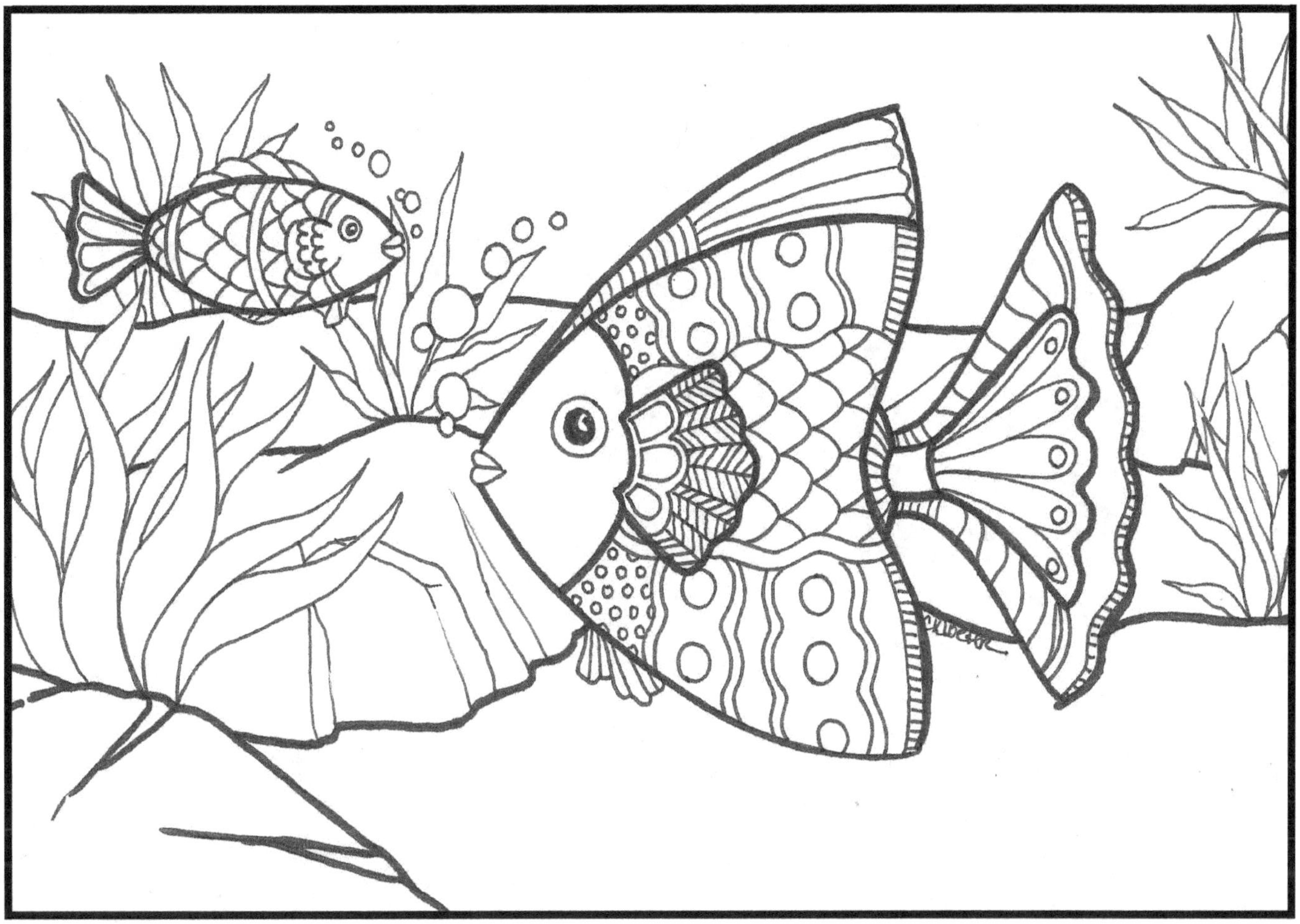

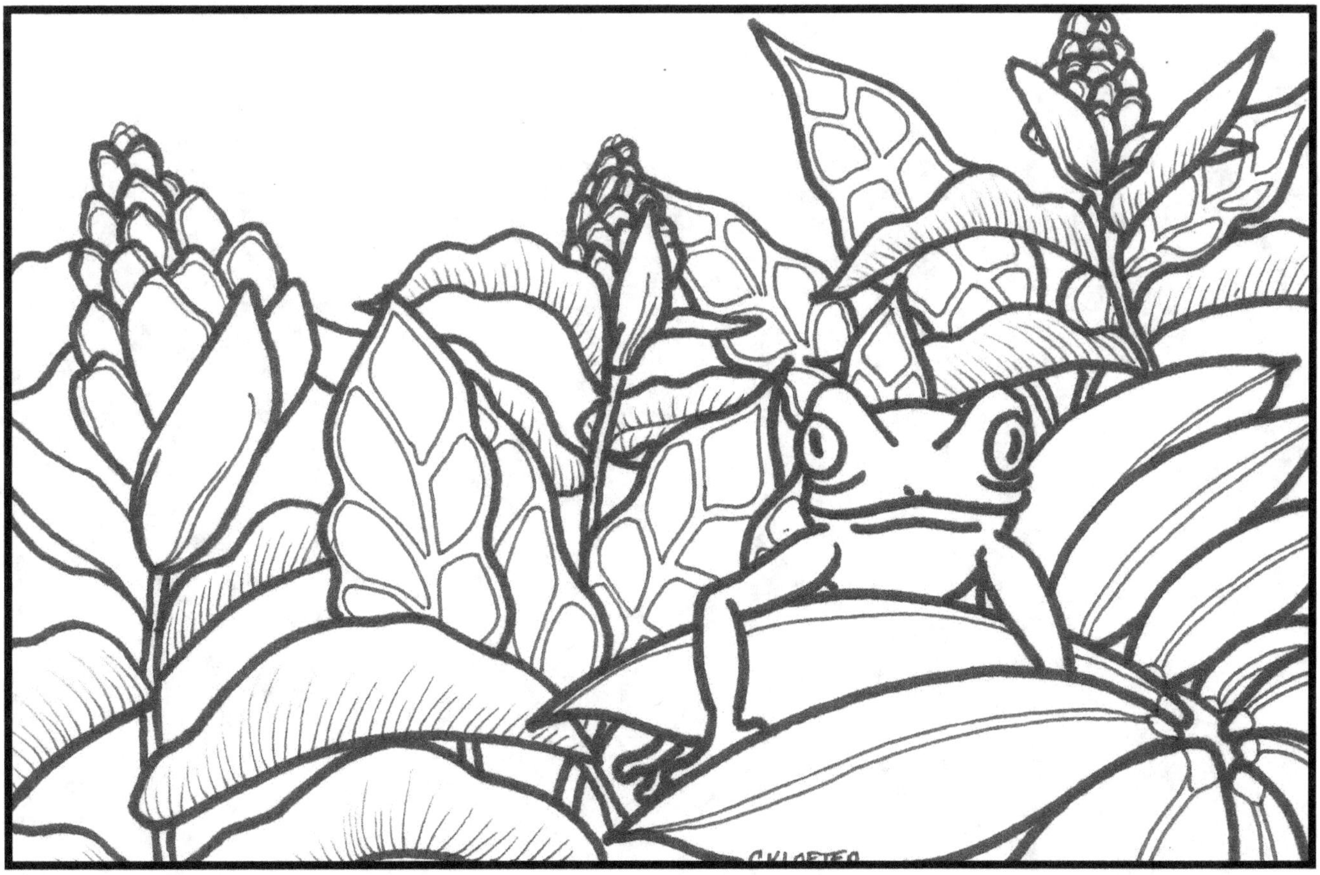

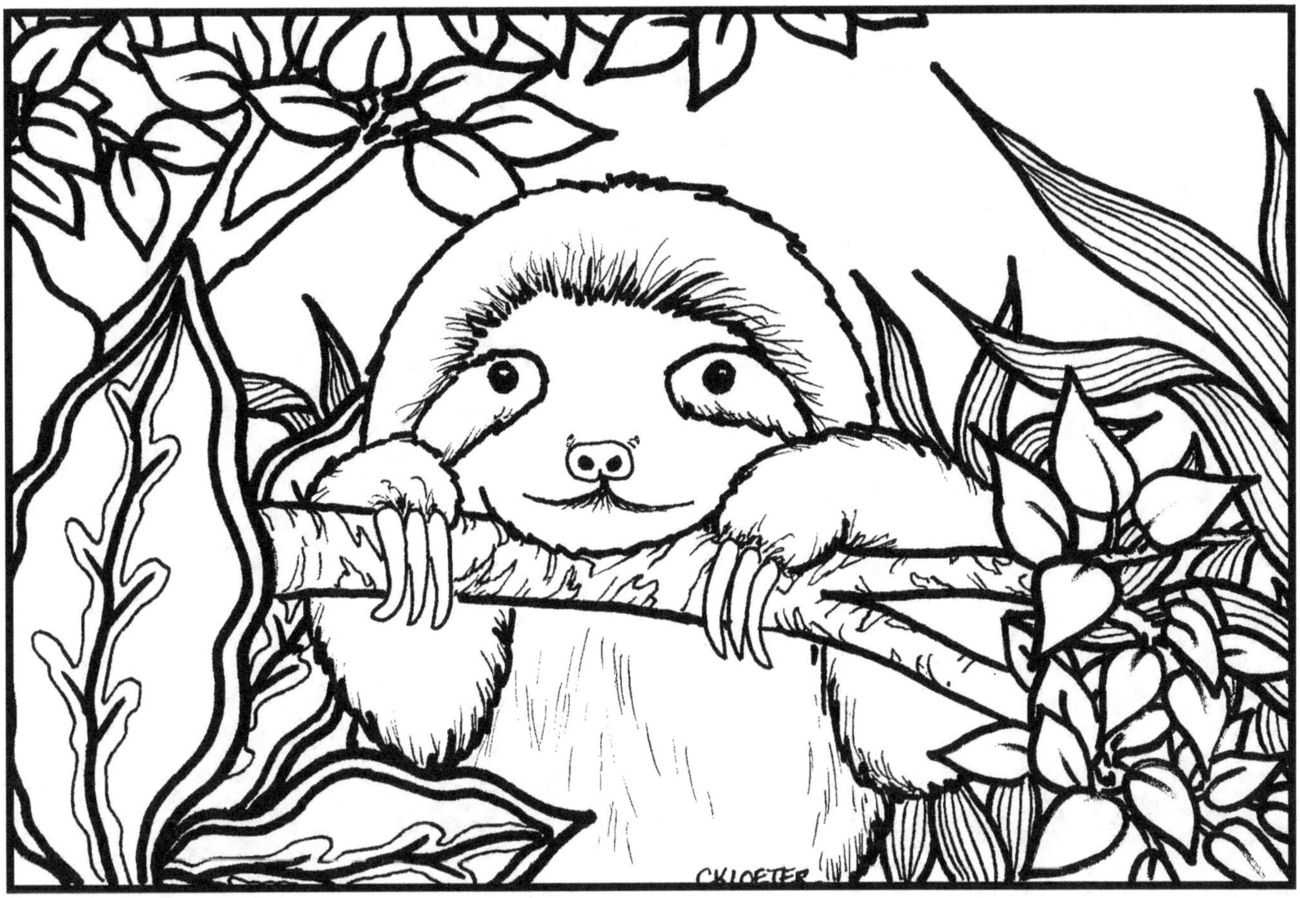
C.KLOETER

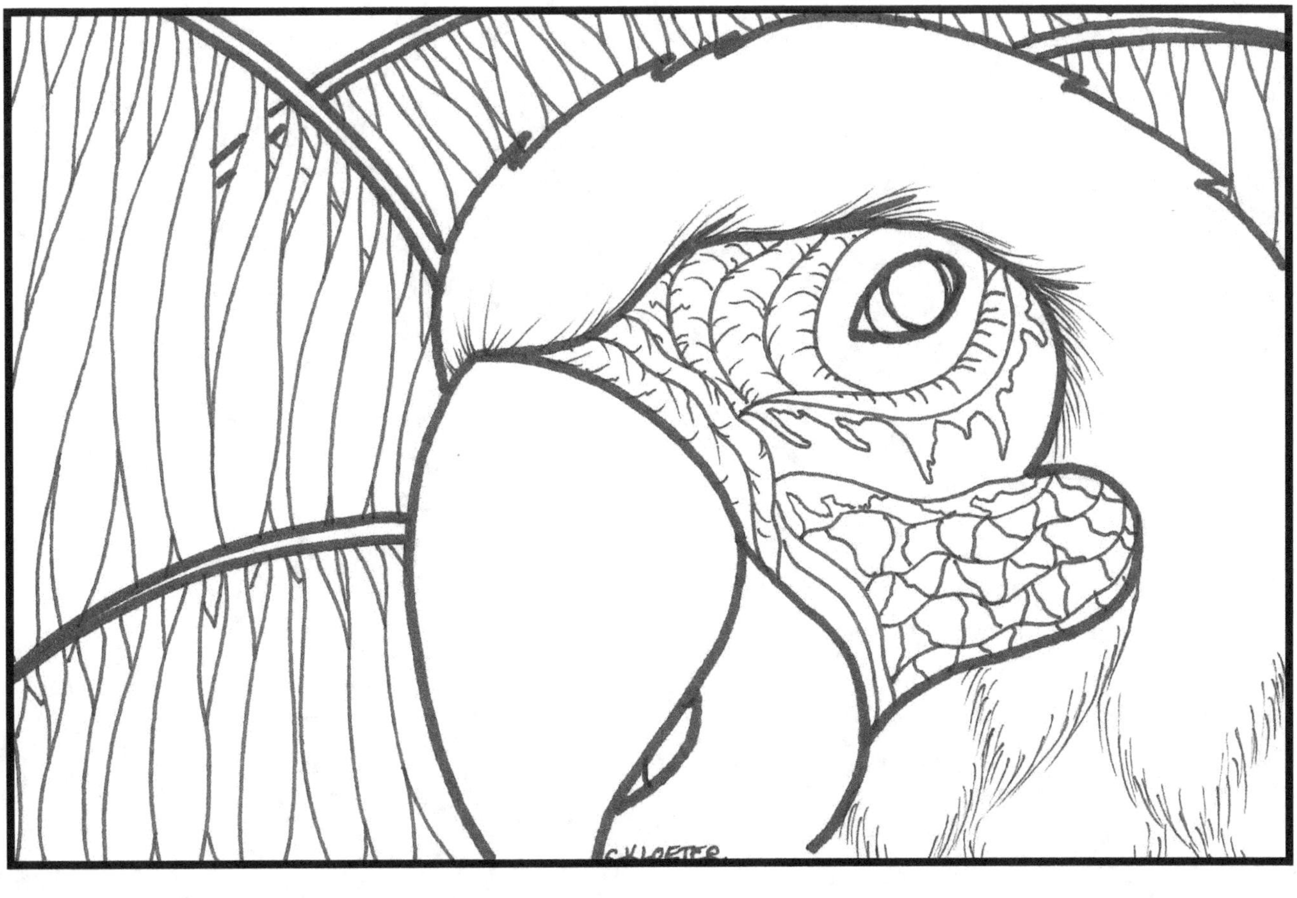
C.KLOETER

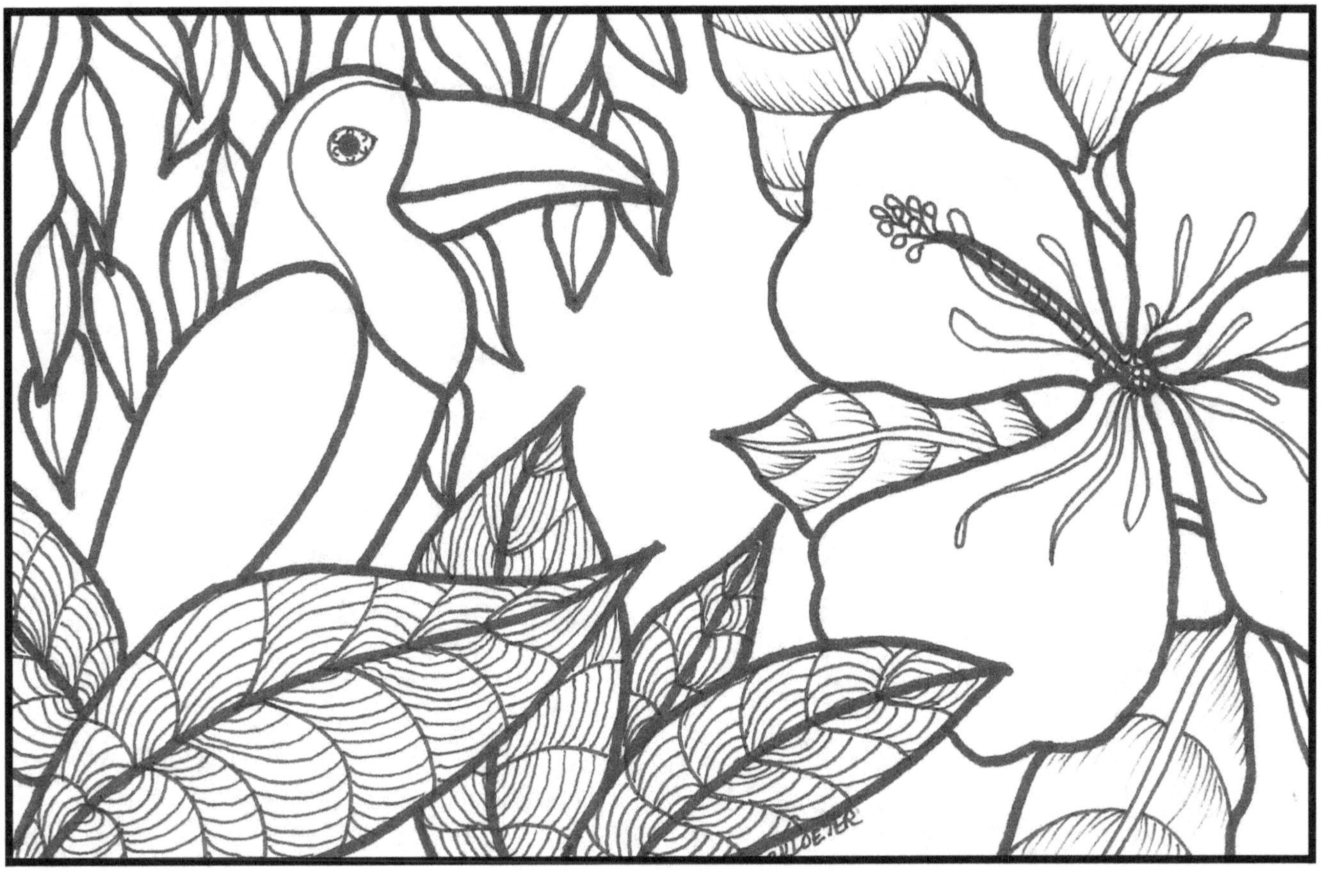

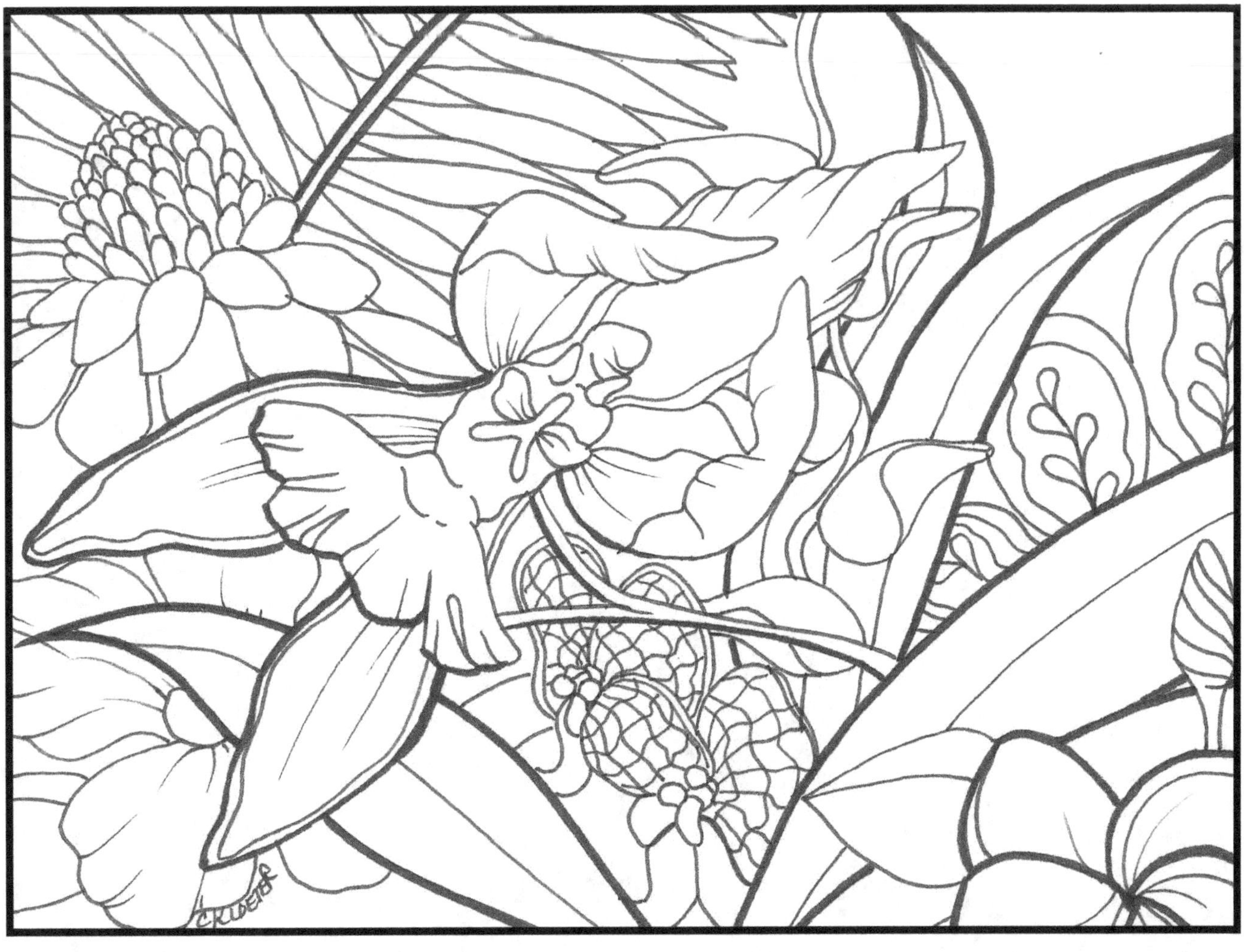

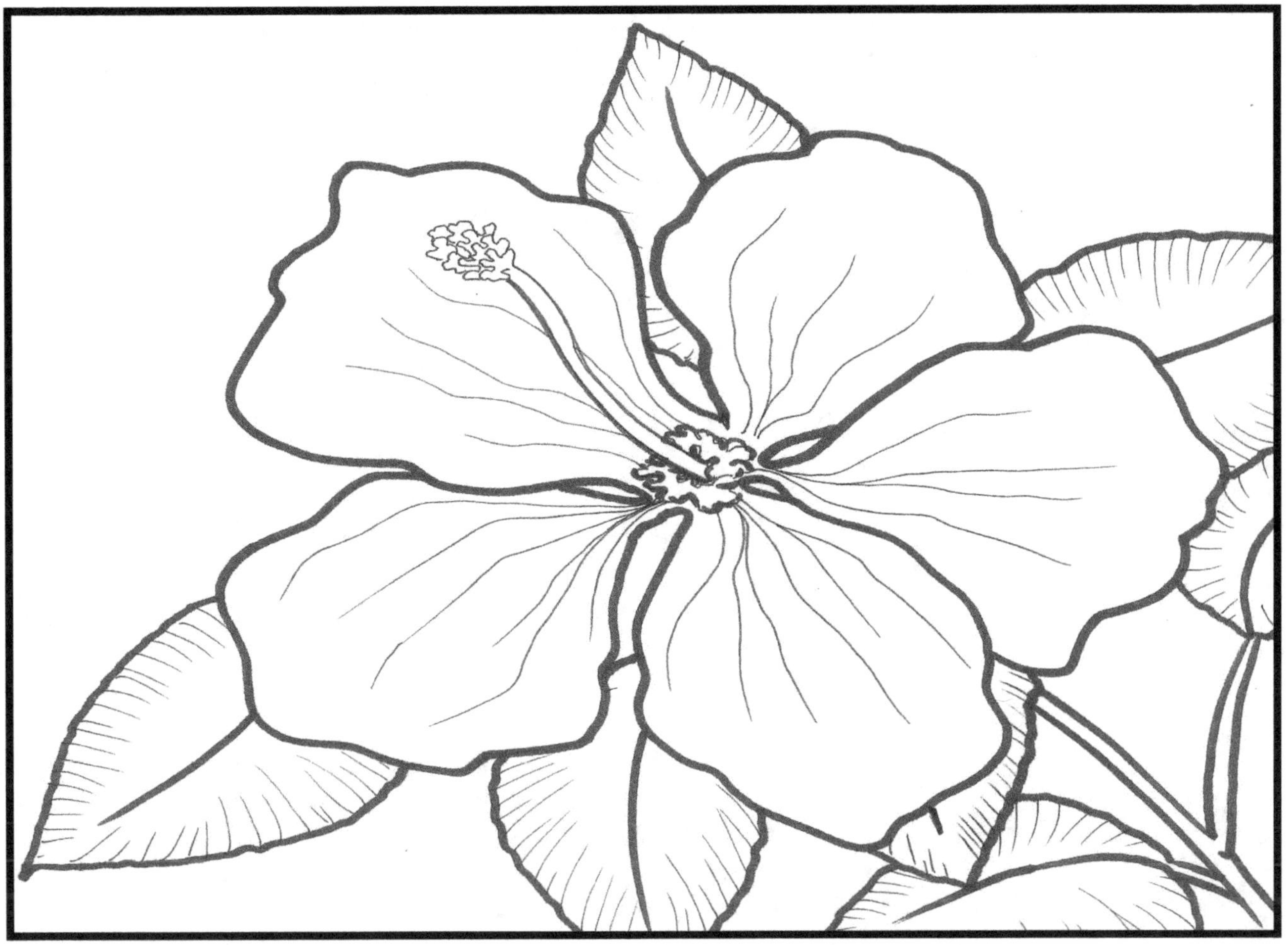

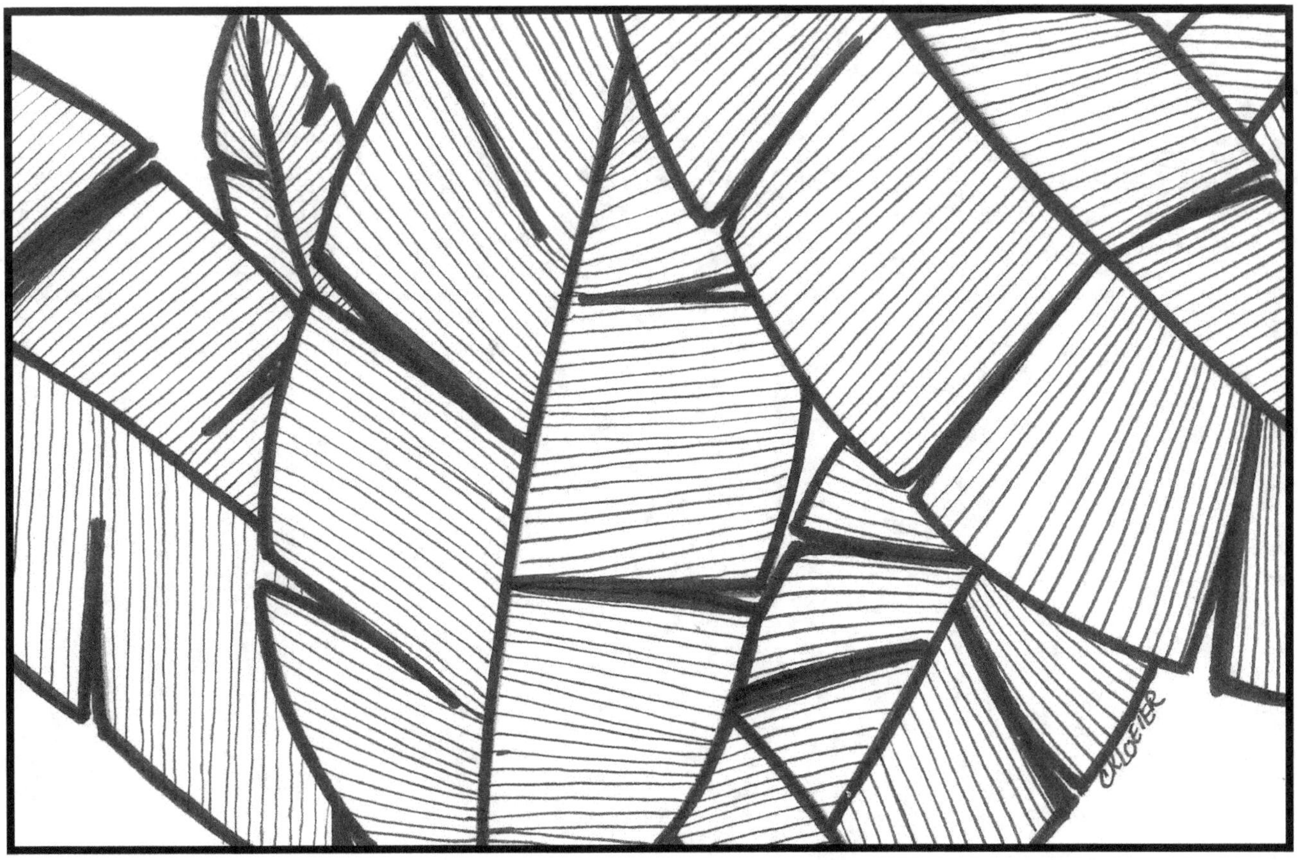

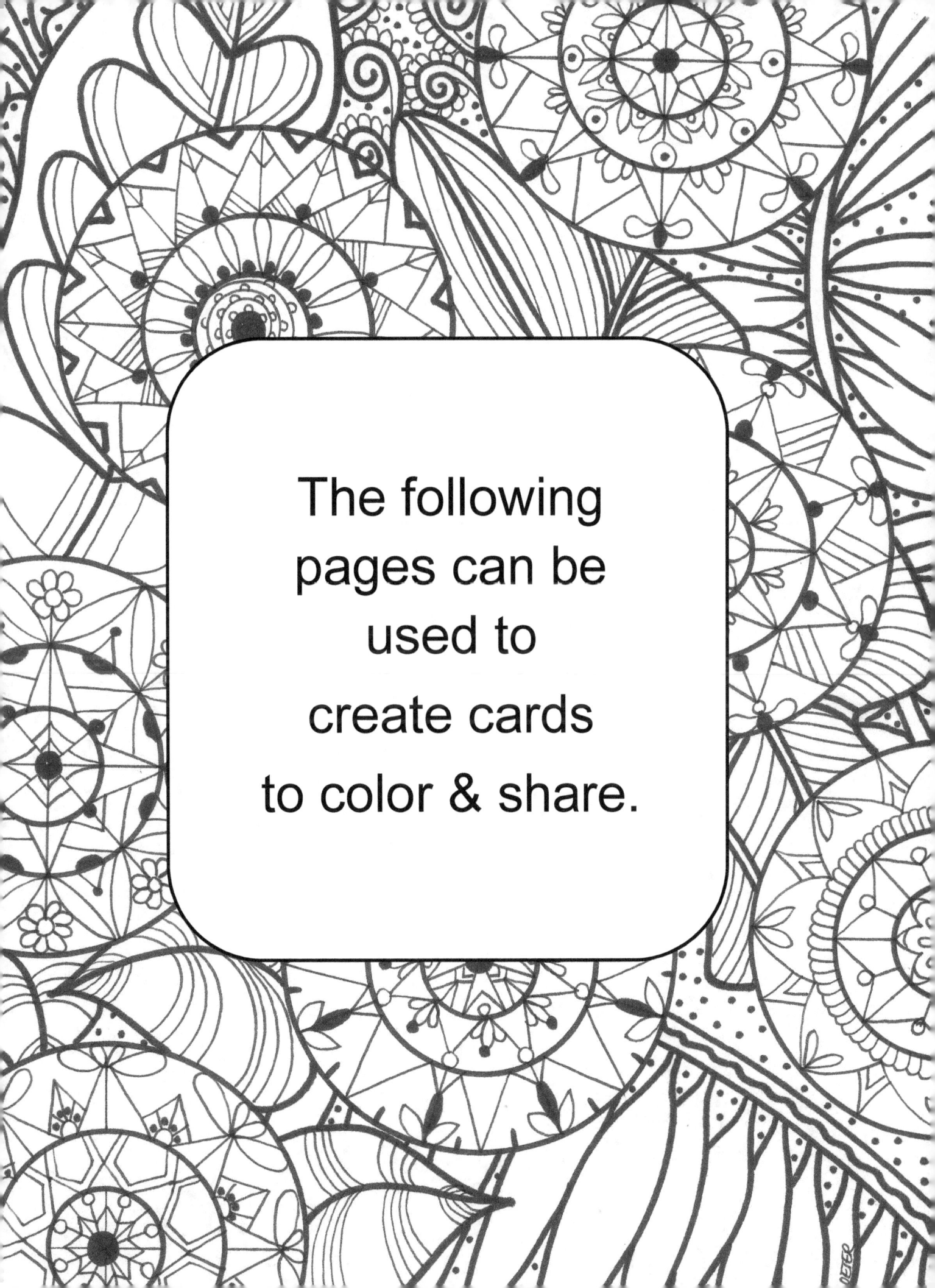

The following
pages can be
used to
create cards
to color & share.

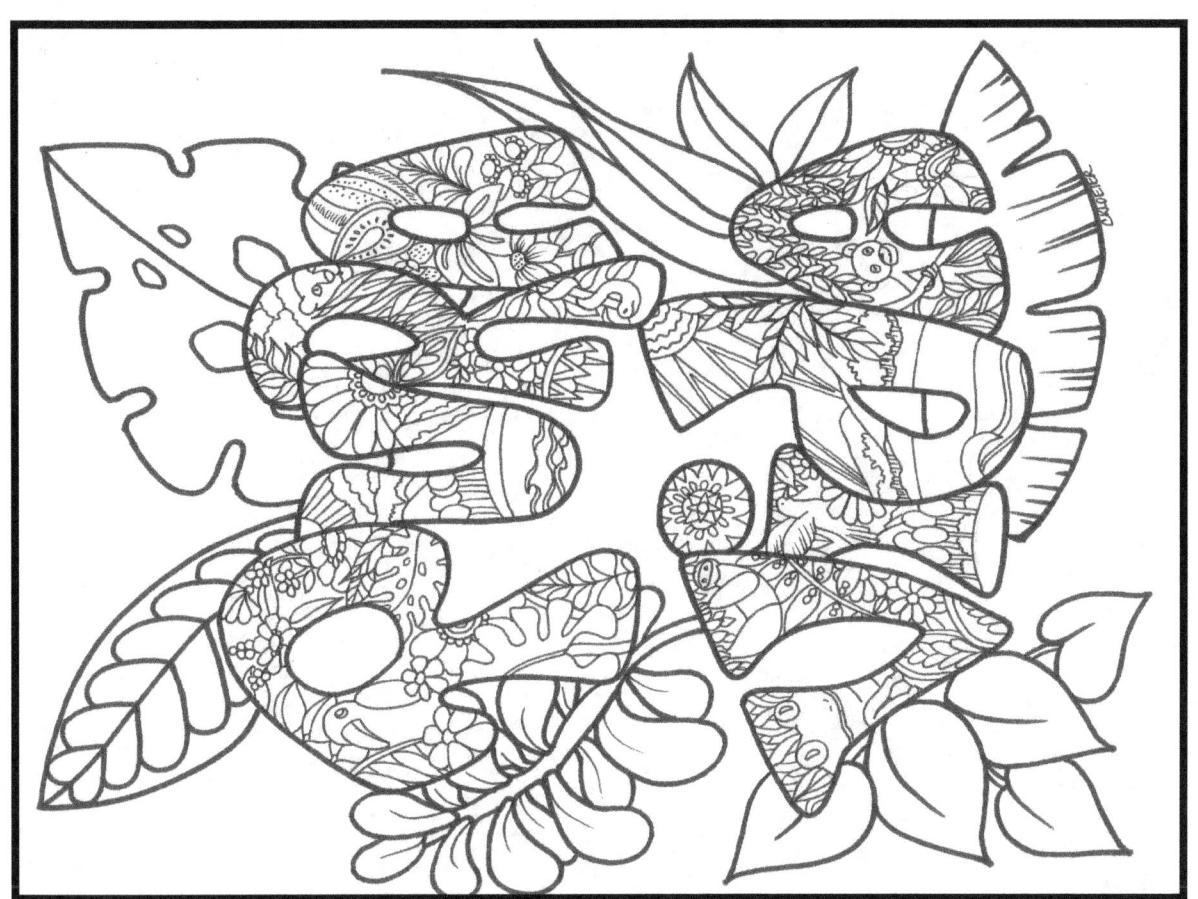

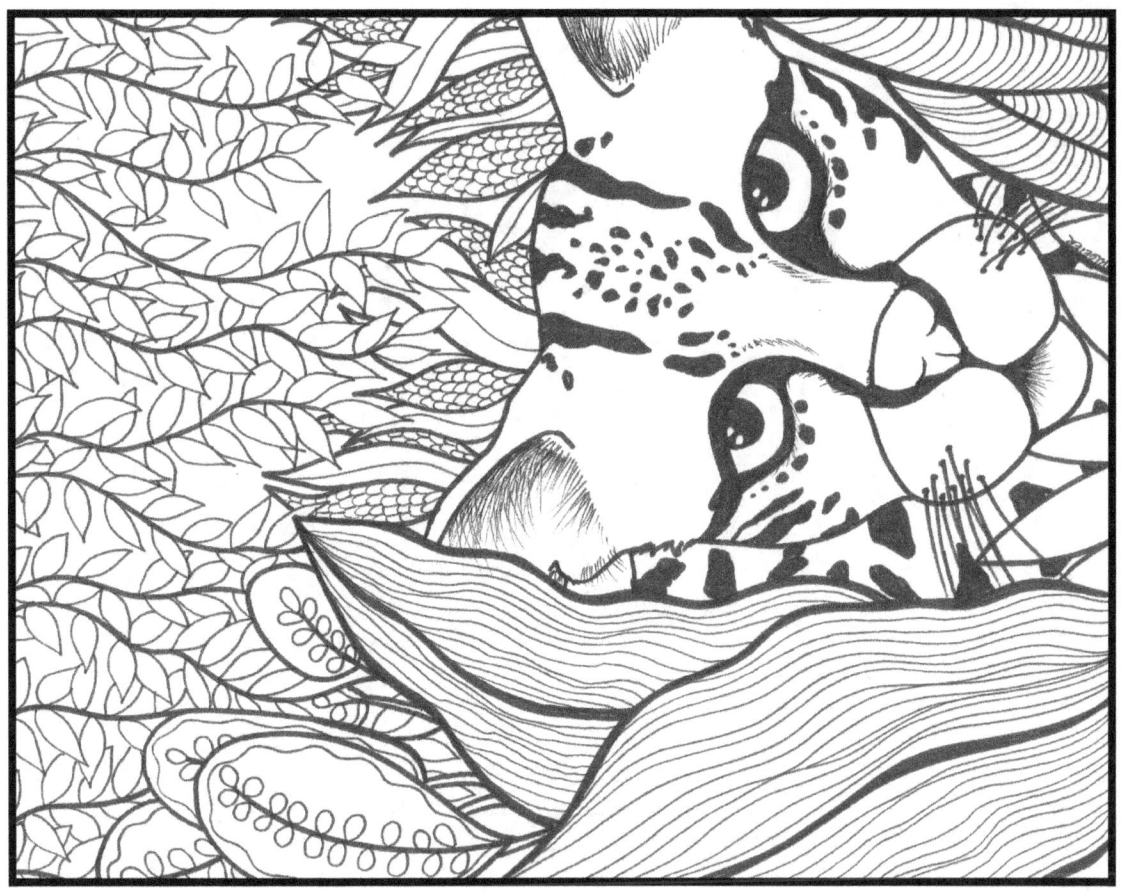

Pura Vida

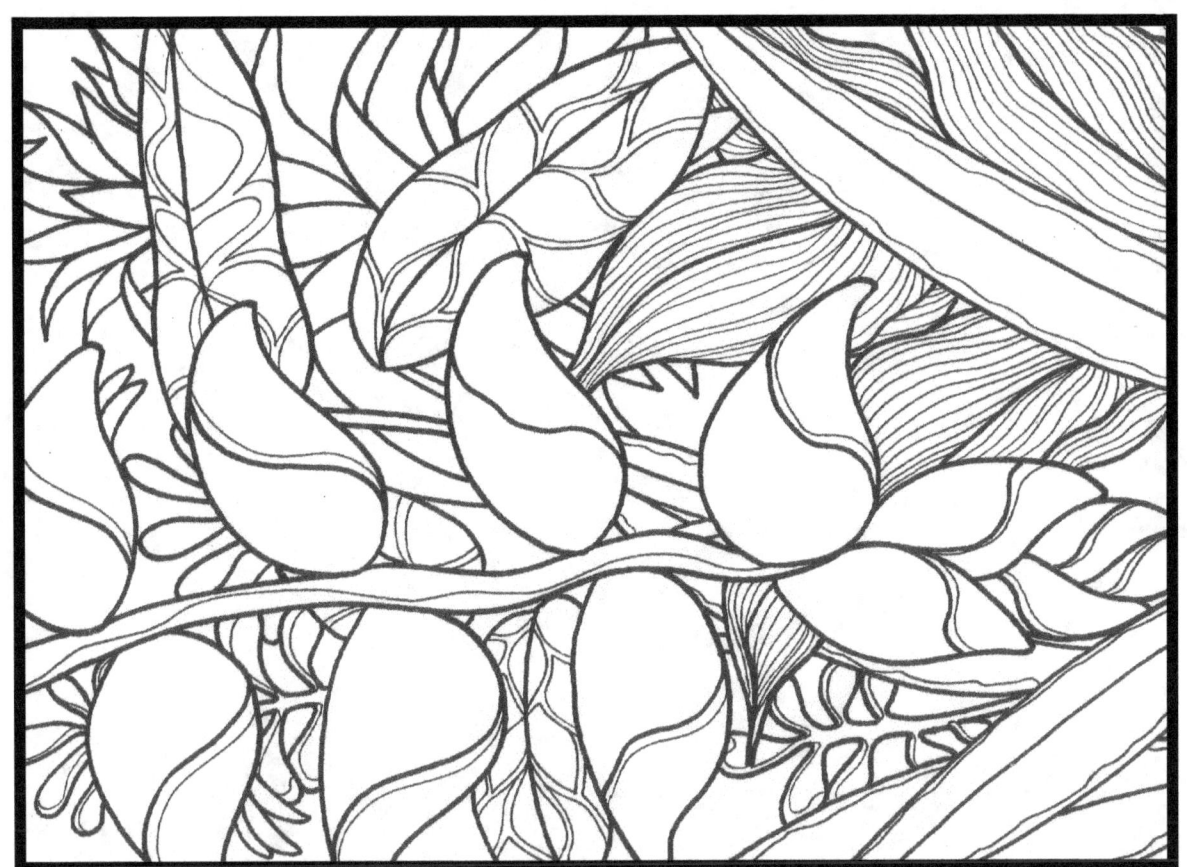

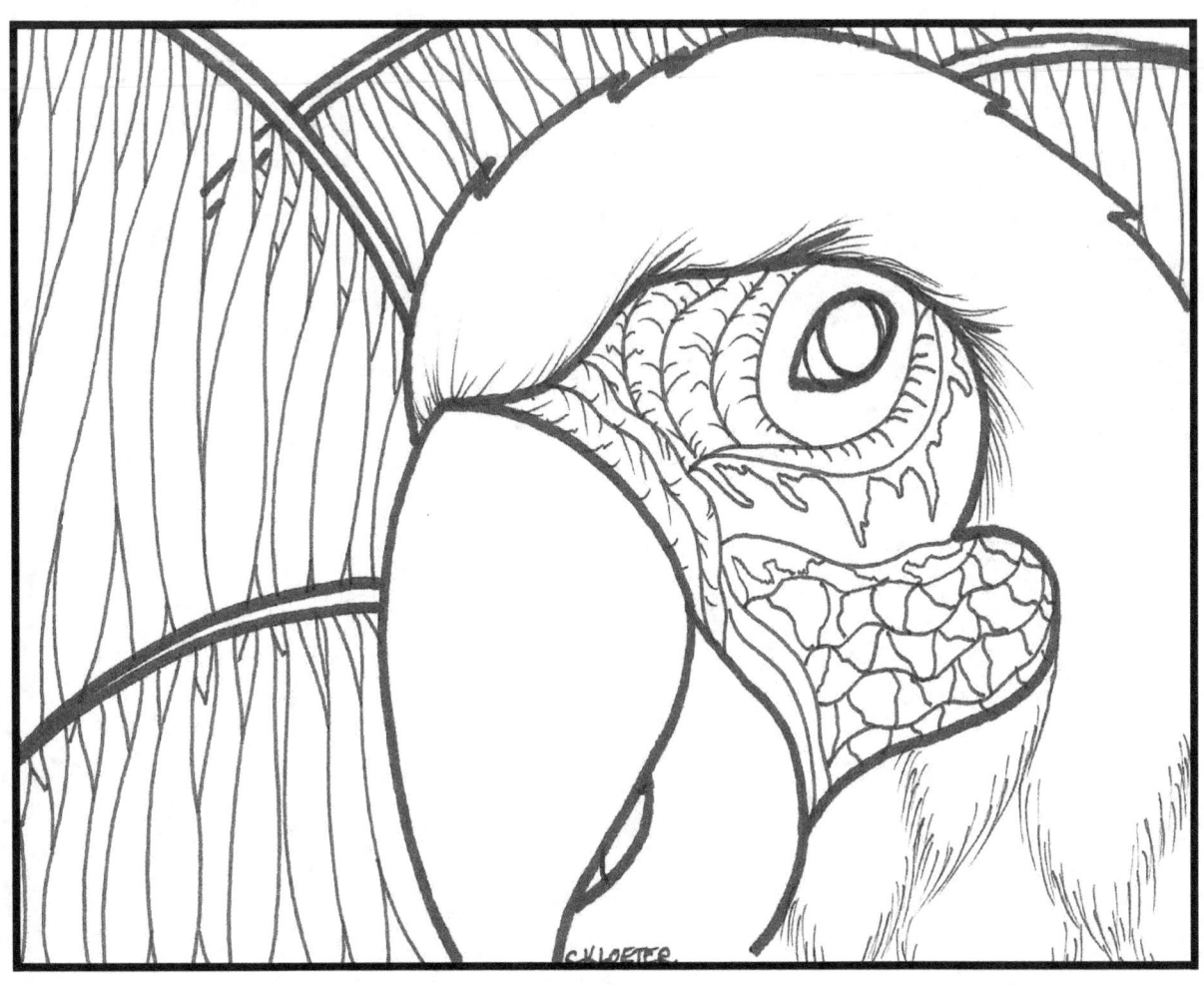

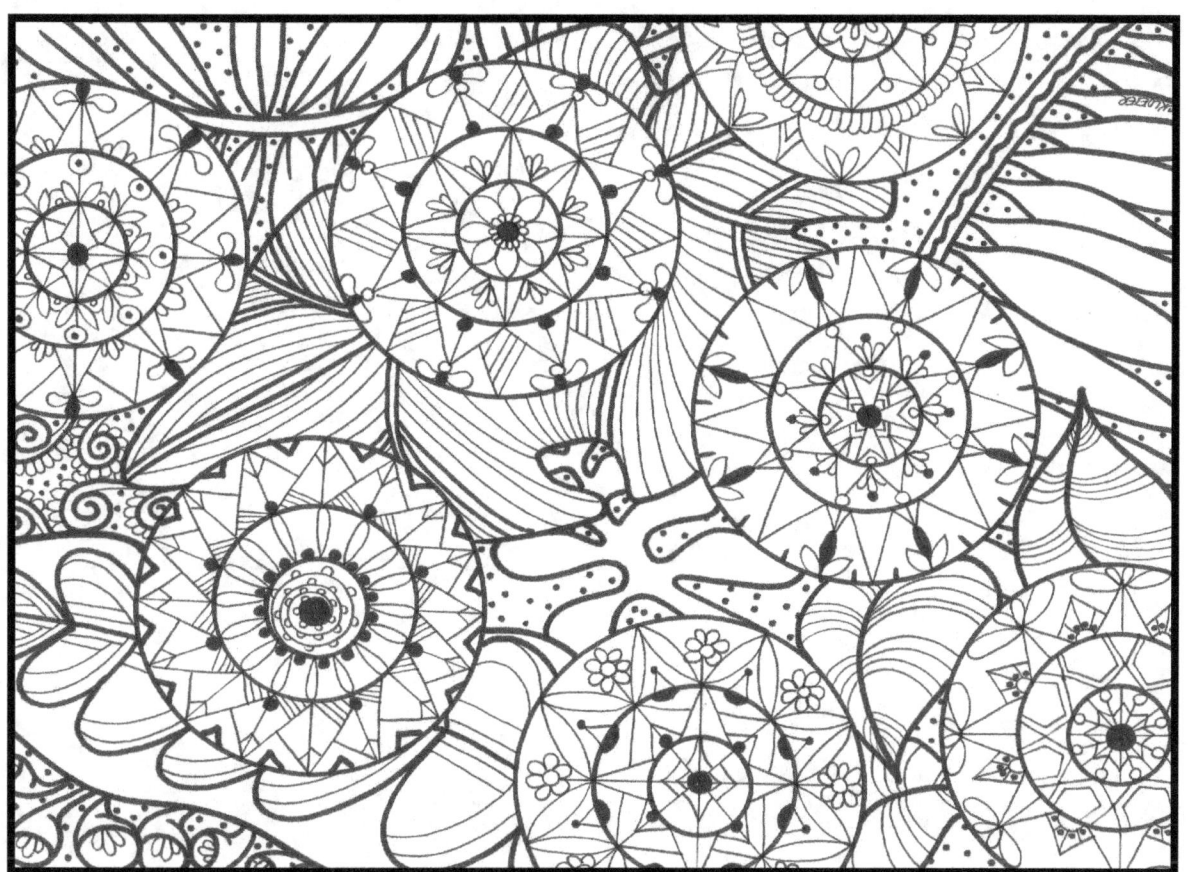

COLOR TEST SHEET

PROTECTION SHEET

Remove from book and place between pages
to protect from marker bleed through.

www.ingramcontent.com/pod-product-compliance
Lightning Source LLC
Chambersburg PA
CBHW081219170526
45165CB00009B/2875